IRRATIONALITY IN INTERNATIONAL CONFRONTATION

Irrationality in International Confrontation

_____ ROBERT MANDEL

CONTRIBUTIONS IN POLITICAL SCIENCE,
NUMBER 185

GREENWOOD PRESS

NEW YORK
WESTPORT, CONNECTICUT
LONDON

Library of Congress Cataloging-in-Publication Data

Mandel, Robert.
  Irrationality in international confrontation.

  (Contributions in political science, ISSN 0147-1066 ;
no. 185)
  Bibliography: p.
  Includes index.
  1. World politics–1945-   . 2. Rationalism.
I. Title. II. Series.
D842.M33 1987   327.1'01   87-7588
ISBN 0-313-25950-X (lib. bdg. : alk. paper)

British Library Cataloguing in Publication Data is available.

Library of Congress Catalog Card Number: 87-7588
ISBN: 0-313-25950-X
ISSN: 0147-1066

First published in 1987

Greenwood Press, Inc.
88 Post Road West, Westport, Connecticut 06881

Printed in the United States of America

The paper used in this book complies with the
Permanent Paper Standard issued by the National
Information Standards Organization (Z39.48-1984).

10 9 8 7 6 5 4 3 2 1

Contents

Preface

This book results from five years of pondering irrationality. Its initial root was a conference paper written in 1981 and presented at the annual national meeting of the International Studies Association in Cincinnati, Ohio, in March 1982. Then a more polished article emerged on the theoretical framework of irrationality and appeared in *Political Psychology* in December 1984. The scrutiny of the case studies occurred well after the development of this framework, allowing time for the author to adjust psychologically to seeing his initial ideas shattered by contrary evidence.

A number of individuals deserve credit for help and encouragement on this project. Alexander George of Stanford University and Whitney Perkins of Brown University (emeritus) were quick to notice flaws in the argumentation of earlier versions of the study, as well as to point out new directions for thinking about the subject. Bill Rottschaefer of Lewis and Clark College asked the important, penetrating philosophical questions. James Swiss of North Carolina State University did his usual erudite job of editing my sometimes convoluted writing style. My wife Annette was an incredible asset, in terms of both helping with ideas for the project and maintaining a positive attitude about it.

Introduction

Irrationality has become one of the common epithets of our times in the international arena. Ronald Reagan in late 1980 labeled Khomeini "irrational" due to the hostage-taking incident and Iran's anti-Western policies. American officials in late 1981 (and many times since then) called Khaddafi "crazy" because of Libya's alleged assassination plot targeted at the President. From Amin's regime in Uganda to Bokassa's reign in the Central African Empire, government leaders stand accused of irrational statements, decisions, and actions. Usually this characterization connotes the most derogatory attributes of the heads-of-state described, often involving total incompetence at the job of running their countries and potential destabilization of the entire international system.

The problem with this label is that it is used with so many different interpretations that it has lost virtually all meaning. Moreover, even when a precise decision emerges, scholars and decision makers alike rarely stop long enough to ask themselves whether irrationality necessarily has to equate with some perverse or pernicious form of human behavior. Quite simply, the term is used thoughtlessly and frivolously in much research and policy in international relations.

The absence of sustained and systematic attention to irrationality leaves a gaping hole in our understanding of key actors and actions in world politics, and is in stark contrast to the rather considerable work on rational models of decision making. Currently there appears to be a rush to apply rational choice models to conflict, and one analyst denies the presence of virtually any irrationality in superpower relations:

> The *apparent* irrationality of such [superpower] conflict stems, I believe, more from the intractable choices the players face in "superpower games" than from actions the players take that may, on occasion, appear irrational. Callous these leaders may be, but stupid they generally are not. . . . We cannot generally blame our present difficulties on the unrestrained recklessness, gross negligence, or simple craziness of unenlightened leaders. By and large, I contend, these leaders act intelligently and prudently to advance their interests.[1]

Nevertheless, most observers agree that international behavior deviates frequently—if not invariably—from standards of rational behavior,[2] though admittedly analysts disagree on what directions the deviations take.[3] These deviations may be increasingly common due to[4] the clash of modernization and traditionalism, growing scarcities and frustrations, extreme single-person regimes, strong ethnic identities, disenchantment with Western culture, and externally supported "non-viable" states.

Rationality is central to Western culture,[5] and as such is one of the primary lenses through which many nations view each other. Because nations tend to find decisions and actions they label as irrational to be the hardest to understand and respond to,[6] there is a pressing need for some theoretical tools to aid in these complex situations.

This book begins to fill the theoretical void surrounding irrationality. The work develops a conceptual framework delineating the nature of irrationality in chapter one, explains research methodology in chapter two, and then in chapters three through six analyzes twelve case studies exhibiting irrationality in international confrontations. The motive for selecting tense confrontations as the context for studying irrationality was the desire to explore its workings in the most critical global circumstances—when stakes are high and national interests are at odds. In light of propositions about the utility and disutility of irrationality from the relevant literature, chapter seven examines the patterns emerging from the case studies about when irrationality seems most and least beneficial. Finally, chapter eight concludes the book with a discussion of the policy implications of the findings. Although the case studies and the analysis focus on the irrationality of national governments in the international arena, the theory draws heavily from interpersonal, intergroup, and organizational studies; some of the insights that emerge may thus be applicable beyond the nation-state, such as to the behavior of terrorist groups.

IRRATIONALITY IN INTERNATIONAL CONFRONTATION

1.

The Nature of Irrationality

This chapter provides the theoretical framework used for studying irrationality in international confrontations. This portion of the book analyzes alternative definitions of this amorphous concept, examines the sources of irrationality in world politics, explores perceptions of irrationality, and considers the meaning of the utility of irrationality. The framework is a preliminary one dealing with a hard-to-grapple-with and elusive topic, introducing a set of interrelated notions ripe for careful scrutiny and re-assessment.

DEFINITIONS OF IRRATIONALITY

As indicated earlier, scores of definitions of irrationality abound: many implicitly express themselves in terms of deviation from some rational norm, but others do not; most focus on process, but others on outcomes; most concentrate on the way people do or do not behave, but others on the way people should or should not behave; and some emphasize contextual criteria, while others simply examine the nature of the arguments and the way in which they are generated or expressed. Philosophers, economists, psychologists, and political scientists all have different paradigms and jargon to bring to bear on the subject.

Out of this definitional morass, four clusters of interpretations of irrationality emerge. Rather than attempting to select one as best, this study finds it more useful to carry all of them through the analysis in order to compare the causes and consequences of the various forms of irrationality. In any case, there appears to be no *a priori* reason to select one of the clusters as superior, and each identifies a different dimension of irrationality. These four dimensions of irrational decisions are (1) incompatibility with policy goals, prevailing consensus, or preferred outcomes; (2) non-comprehensive search-and-evaluation; (3) inconsistency of statements and/or actions; and (4) non-dispassionate style. Classifying these four dimensions as reflecting irrationality implies only that they involve deviations from rational norms, not that they lack significant forethought.

The first dimension—incompatibility of a decision with policy goals, prevailing consensus, or preferred outcomes—encompasses considerable variation in the meaning of irrationality. A decision may clash with any one of these three yardsticks, or there may be internal contradictions among the three that seem to make conformity to all impossible. For example, an individual bureaucrat's policy goals may clash with the prevailing consensus in the society as a whole (though this clash is less commonly identified as irrational), or the goals and consensus may support a policy that produces undesired outcomes. George[1] examines the importance of goals and consensus through his discussion of "quality" and "acceptability" of decisions, and he notes that there is often a tradeoff dilemma between these two. Both of these criteria for judging irrationality may involve moral and ethical constraints[2] and a nation's socio-cultural ethos.[3] Howard[4] best explains the third incompatibility—with preferred outcomes—by asserting that a decision is irrational if other decisions exist which have foreseeable consequences that are preferable to it (in the eyes of the decision maker). An ecological example of this association of rationality with desired outcomes is evolutionary adaptation, in which "irrational" adaptation or non-adaptation seems to lead to extinction, while "rational" adaptation leads to species growth.[5] This last notion, which involves great controversy, considers the level of success of a decision's predicted impact to be more important in determining irrationality than the manner in which the decision is reached.

The second dimension—non-comprehensive search-and-evaluation—is probably the most common definition of an irrational decision. Here the notion clearly relates to an ideal standard of rationality, called the "analytic," "utility-maximization," or "synoptic" model.[6] In this model decision makers carefully and systematically clarify values and objectives, identify a wide range of policy alternatives designed to meet these ends, seek out information and opinions about these alternatives, and then evaluate each of the alternatives in terms of the gains and losses involved. This cost-benefit analysis, which involves maximizing the expected utility of the decision makers, usually incorporates the short-term and long-term advantages of each policy alternative for each of the relevant actors affected by the decision. This system places a premium on prudent management of time and other policy-making resources[7] and on the technical proficiency of the decision maker. There is often a tradeoff here between the comprehensiveness and the efficiency of the process. Some writers[8] link this rational search-and-evaluation procedure to the scientific method, but others[9] claim that scientific procedures are too rigorous to apply to foreign policy making. Irrational decisions (or those with "bounded rationality") would be those that in some way fail to meet these demanding process specifications. Three well-known deviations from this rational model are satisficing,[10] disjointed incrementalism,[11] and groupthink.[12]

The third dimension—inconsistency of statements and/or actions—does not look at external criteria to judge a decision's irrationality. Instead, the focus is on the absence of internal logical consistency. This more deductive or axiomatic approach calls a decision irrational if there seem to be logical inconsistencies in policy making between relevant past and present statements, past and present actions, or statements and actions. This stress on valid inference, which some term "epistemic rationality,"[13] is problematic in that there are many forms of logical consistency that differ across cultures and even across time and policy issues.[14] Certainly a discrepancy exists between linguistic consistency[15] and substantive consistency. Moreover, Simon[16] points out that a standard of "no conclusions without premises" faces difficulties because (1) the initial premises are often "not derived from logic but simply induced from empirical observations, or even more simply posited"; and (2) the rules of inference are "also introduced by fiat and are not the products of reason." In the foreign policy context, inconsistency concerns raise the oft-asked question about whether lying by national leaders is rational.

The last dimension—a non-dispassionate style of policy making—is perhaps the most controversial aspect of irrational decisions. Generally this refers to the entrance of emotionalism into decision making. Simon[17] shows that emotionalism can create a narrowed focus of attention that is not necessarily warranted. Etheredge[18] points out that the degree of emotional involvement by career diplomats in the foreign policy realm is at least as great as that of domestic professionals: "Clearly there is no good case to be made that the norms or rationality within foreign policy elites systematically prevent emotional engagement in their area of expertise." Janis and Mann[19] link this pervasive lack of impartiality to the "hot cognition" syndrome. Morgan[20] mentions emotional impulsiveness as one of the key irrationalities involved in deterrence. This dimension uses emotional style more as a symptom of the presence of irrationality than as a demonstration of irrationality itself, and is the only one of the four clusters of irrationality to stress affective rather than cognitive elements of a decision. The implicit assumption here is that rationality involves a detached, machine-like mode of analysis. There is some reason to believe[21] that acting emotionally on the basis of fears and desires is just as pervasive and significant in international relations as simplifying the environment through relying on the inertia of past experience or expectations.

In none of these dimensions is there a precise threshold identifiable between rationality and irrationality, and indeed a continuum appears necessary. Figure 1 displays such a continuum, and it shows that irrationality can occur at both ends of the spectrum of fluctuation in foreign policy: "stick-in-the-mud" irrationality often reflects cautious incremental decisions, while "daredevil" irrationality often reflects dramatic and brash decisions. In terms of the rational standards implied by the four definitional dimensions, both stick-in-the-mud and daredevil decisions reject appropriate adaptation to the external environment: stick-in-the-mud policy fluctuates too little to cope with changing external circumstances (underreactive), while daredevil policy fluctuates too much to deal with them (overreactive). Naturally, the rational systematic evaluator may choose to undertake either status quo or aggressive policies; but the pre-

Figure 1
Rationality-Irrationality Continuum

LOW FLUCTUATION IN FOREIGN POLICY	MEDIUM FLUCTUATION IN FOREIGN POLICY	HIGH FLUCTUATION IN FOREIGN POLICY
Sluggish and Stagnant Foreign Policy	Coherent and Calculated Foreign Policy	Rash and Reckless Foreign Policy
Stick-In-The-Mud	Systematic Evaluator	Daredevil
IRRATIONAL	RATIONAL	IRRATIONAL

sumption is that such decisions would reflect careful analysis of available information and prevailing conditions, precisely tuned to the situation at hand. The essence of the stick-in-the-mud/daredevil distinction is thus an unwillingness/inability to avoid tiny and inadequate policy adjustments in the first case, and to avoid monumental and overdramatic policy shifts in the second case. This distinction is complicated by (1) states exhibiting combinations of stick-in-the-mud and daredevil irrationality at different times; (2) states regularly altering foreign policies according to predictable (and even cyclical) patterns; and (3) the external circumstances confronting a state themselves often being the product of ephemeral decisions by other states.

Irrationality can occur at various stages in the policy making process. In most cases , irrationality occurs in some of the stages but not in others. In the first stage, identifying the problem, decision makers could miss a crucial issue or exaggerate the importance of a non-issue; in the second stage, gathering of information, they could distort or ignore accessible information; in the third stage, processing of information, they could perform an inadequate cost-benefit analysis due to inappropriate articulation of values, incomplete identification of options and actors, or erroneous assessment of advantages and disadvantages; in the fourth stage, formulating the decision, they could make a choice which ignores or contradicts the results of the information processing; in the fifth stage, implementing the action, they could behave in a way that ignores or contradicts the stated decision; and in the sixth stage, responding to feedback, they could distort or ignore external inputs.

In light of these categorization schemes, foreign policy may exhibit varying degrees of irrationality. The most irrational behavior would probably fit the criteria of all four dimensions and be present in all six stages of the policy process, while the least irrational behavior might fit just one dimension at just one policy-making stage. Of course, each occurrence of irrationality is not equally important: for example, irrationality at the problem identification stage may be more critical in terms of overall policy effects than irrationality at the action implementation stage; and irrationality at the strategic level may be more important than at the tactical level. A decision which is rational according to some definitions or at some stages can still be classified as irrational if it fails to match the rational standards elsewhere. If taken to an extreme, this approach could consider virtually all behavior in the international arena to be irrational. No foreign policy decision has ever really met all of the criteria of rationality at all of the stages of decision making.

Presenting three different schemes for classifying irrationality may appear to be a bit convoluted, but these taxonomies seem essential to pin down this mercurial concept. Figure 2 combines these classification systems to provide an overall picture of irrationality in international relations.

The focus of this study is on those international confrontations which display "significant" irrationality, in which there are major deviations from the standards of rationality. More specifically, the emphasis is on clashes among states where considerable evidence points to the presence of more than one dimension of irrationality during more than one stage of the policy-making process. The presence of such evidence usually means that the deviation in the stick-in-the-mud or daredevil direction has been blatant and large—not just slight but severe sluggishness or recklessness in foreign affairs. While such deviations are not conducive to precise measurement or the establishment of a fixed threshold, they do reflect the weight of international and internal public opinion and prestige. Encompassing more than one irrationality dimension and more than one policy-making stage ensures that the deviations are not so contained and isolated that they have little overall importance in the context of the decision or action; in other words, the emphasized deviations seem likely to have spillover effects and a pervasive influence over the entire confrontation.

SOURCES OF IRRATIONALITY

Detecting when and how irrationality surfaces in foreign policy is as tricky as defining the concept itself. This study distinguishes between the broad underlying roots of irrationality and the more specific conditions under which irrationality is particularly likely to surface.

Three broad underlying roots of irrationality are the nature of the individual decision maker, of the decision-making environment,

Figure 2
Definitional Context of Irrationality

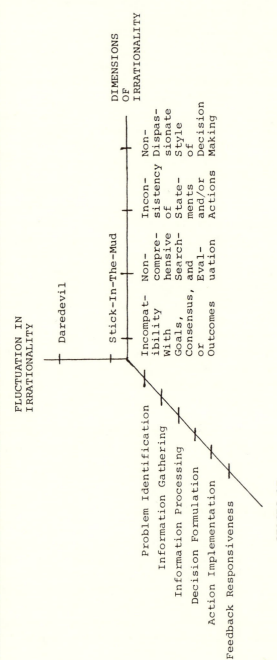

and of the specific decision. The first involves each decision maker's idiosyncratic personality traits[22] and technical proficiency.[23] As Dougherty and Pfaltzgraff[24] point out, "For many decades, the Western intellectual's faith in the essential rationality of human behavior (inherited from the Enlightenment) has steadily disintegrated." Many analysts now consider human frailty in decision making to be the rule rather than the exception, and emphasize the constraints on individual human reason rather than its potentialities. The second source involves (1) the bureaucratic environment— the organizational roles and the type of government structure;[25] and (2) the societal context—the level of development of the society[26] and the type of culture.[27] The relevant socialization of the decision maker primarily stems from the two environments, and they to a large extent constrain the range of choice in thought and action for any particular confrontation. The final source of irrationality involves the level of information and time pressure present in the confrontation[28] and the salience of the confrontation issues, particularly in terms of the threat to vital national interests.[29] These last characteristics, which reveal whether or not a crisis is at hand, are critical in determining which aspects of the individual decision maker and of the bureaucratic and social environments are brought to bear in the particular confrontation.

The specific conditions under which irrationality seems most likely in foreign policy flow naturally from these three broad roots. Turning first to the nature of the individual decision maker, Janis and Mann[30] show that a lack of detachment can lead to "hyper-vigilance" or panic among decision makers. Often this involves the use of "bolstering," artificially magnifying the attractiveness of the preferred alternative:[31] a radical fanatic might bolster risky options, in line with daredevil irrationality; while a traditional reactionary might bolster stand-pat.options, in line with stick-in-the-mud irrationality.[32] One form of irrationality which is especially prominent here is "black-and-white" thinking, in which decision makers view issues in all-or-nothing terms.[33] A critical question, posed by Verba,[34] concerns these personality influences on irrationality: when will decision makers choose international relations as the outlet for personal emotional needs? Although some research[35] has emerged on this question, it seems difficult to determine when policy makers isolate these needs from their professional role and when they inject these needs into this role, for these conditions relate to the ever-changing overlap between personal and national aspirations across the range of issues considered. Moving to non-personality aspects of individual decision makers, there are four aspects of a lack of technical proficiency: (1) physiological limitations[36] on a bureaucrat's ability to reason—to identify and analyze information, policy goals, and policy alternatives—based on biological constraints in our basic cognitive structures; (2) a lack of training in the skills of sound decision making;[37] (3) over-reliance on intuition and creativity in decision making at the expense of systematic thinking;[38] and (4) non-idiosyncratic patterns of perceptual distortion[39] such as cognitive consistency and ethnocentrism. The perceptual distortions are pervasive across individuals and bureaucratic and social settings, and so continually inject irrationality regardless of context; but the physiological limits, reliance on intuition, and level of training vary considerably, and so may introduce significant differentiation in the level of technical proficiency and hence of irrationality.

Turning to the nature of the decision-making environment, Verba[40] argues that irrationality is more likely to appear among decision makers with low levels of influence and responsibility than among those with high levels, due to the personal anxiety of officials with little influence and to the inhibitions against irrationality at positions of high responsibility (and accountability). While this contention is controversial, Janis and Mann[41] confirm that low responsibility can cause decision makers to deny accountability for their actions and to attribute choices to external pressures. If the government is small and highly centralized, then daredevil irrationality seems more likely among top leaders because of the absence of checks-and-balances or input from below and the exclusive significance of the whims of the autocrat; whereas if the government is highly decentralized, then stick-in-the-mud irrationality seems more likely because of the bureaucratic inertia built in by having to satisfy all of the policy-making constituencies as well as the mood of the electorate.[42] Similarly, developing countries seem more prone to daredevil irrationality and developed countries to stick-in-the-mud irrationality, because the former have less to lose (in terms of international influence), have more non status-quo global objectives, have more emotionally charged colonial legacies,[43] and have smaller bureaucracies affording a higher level of individual control.[44] However, the developed nations' power can certainly be conducive to an unrestrained, non-self-assessing irrationality all of its own. The less the society values rationality (and the more it values "tradition"), the greater are the irrational influences on decision making.[45] Furthermore, a society with ill-defined goals, major internal disagreements on goals, or frequent changes in goals over time appears to be ripe for irrationality: for example, inconsistency of statements and/or actions is probably most evident in pluralist societies, due to the openness and multiplicity of key actors, and for similar reasons such inconsistency is difficult for such societies to limit or control.[46]

Finally, the nature of the decision itself is critical. Irrationality seems most likely when decision makers have little information about the issue involved or about the motives, decisions, or actions of other states. George[47] indicates that under uncertainty decision makers may resort to "defensive procrastination"—relating to stick-in-the-mud irrationality—in order to escape from the unpleasantness of the situation. Savage[48] confirms this finding by showing that when probabilities of outcomes are unknown, an official may make choices that minimize the regret felt if these decisions turn out to be wrong. When so little information exists that a situation is highly ambiguous, Steinbruner[49] asserts that it is easier for decision makers to avoid the "reality principle" and not recognize critical tradeoffs because of the flexibility of interpretation permitted by the unstructured situation. High time pressure promotes irrationality because decision makers consider a reduced number of alternatives and give priority to those previously formulated,[50] linking again to the stick-in-the-mud syndrome. Under time pressure bureaucrats may also exaggerate outside threat and focus only on immediate consequences of decisions, creating more pressure to act hastily.[51] When time pressure increases the likelihood that a .policy maker converts a false alarm into war,[52] then daredevil irrationality seems sure to follow. Last, the feeling of being "backed against the wall" and possibly losing on a vital issue can lead to irrationality in foreign policy. Moffitt and Stagner[53] find that threat-induced anxiety increases the chances of cognitive closure and perceptual rigidity, tendencies associated with bureaucratic inertia and stick-in-the-mud irrationality. Pruitt[54] contends that high threat can lead to distorted perceptions of evidence and lead to "possibilitic thinking," in which future events which are rationally only possible appear probable. Thus political-military crises combining high uncertainty, high time pressure, and high outside threat seem most likely to lead to policy irrationality. While Morgan[55] indicates that crises may sometimes promote rationality, the apparent discrepancy is reconciled by the growing agreement[56] that a curvilinear relationship exists between level of crisis and decision-making performance: mild crises may make performance more rational while severe crises may not.

PERCEPTION OF IRRATIONALITY

Having seen the general roots of irrationality and the specific conditions when it emerges, an important question remains: when do decision makers perceive irrationality in international confrontations? The most common pattern is for states to view themselves and others as rational because assuming irrationality "would make any attempt to persuade, bargain, or negotiate wasteful or dangerous."[57] But there are, as examples in the introduction illustrate, conditions when policy makers perceive irrationality in others, if not in themselves. Part of the complexity here is that the criteria used by one nation to judge another's rationality may be quite different from those used in judging itself. The "actor observer" distinction[58] may apply here, claiming that when a nation views itself (the "actor" perspective) it attributes its behavior to stimuli inherent in the external situation, while when viewing other nations (the "observer" perspective) it attributes their behavior to internal "stable dispositions." A state seems particularly likely to perceive irrationality in other states when they are political enemies,[59] when they have significantly different cultures or values or forms of government,[60] or when they have a past history of failure in the eyes of the perceiver.[61] Other previously mentioned conditions, such as other nations' inconsistencies of statements and/or actions and their lack of clarification of motives, can also clearly lead to perceptions of irrationality. Because states seem to perceive irrationality in themselves much less often than it actually occurs, it appears that considerable self-deception transpires in the international system.[62] The most common perceptual patterns seem to be for states to accuse each other of daredevil rather than stick-in-the-mud irrationality, because of the former's flagrant visibility; and for developed nations to accuse developing nations of irrationality more than the reverse, due to the general condescension of the North toward the South.

The question of perceived versus genuine irrationality is central because, when examining the consequences of irrationality, some contend that the image is more important than the reality. As Howard[63] points out, a state may pretend to be irrational while in fact pursuing a rational policy. In this case, where a state is consciously choosing to use strategies associated with irrationality as the best means to achieve desired ends, the state may indeed not be acting irrationally at all. But to the perceiver or target of such moves, unaware of the extent to which they are the product of rational choice, there is no functional distinction between genuine and manipulated irrationality (as long as the moves appear irrational). The level of subtle sophistication needed for false projections of irrationality does not seem common.

UTILITY OF IRRATIONALITY

It is this study's normative contention that under some conditions irrationality is actually preferable to rationality in foreign policy. "Preferable" means increasing the effectiveness of government decision makers, and by extension their nation, in areas they deem important relating to national interests. In the foreign policy context, irrationality would be preferable if it reduced the perceived likelihood of failure and increased that of success by overcoming the inadequacies of rational approaches to a particular situation. Thus this is a subjective interpretation, making no direct claims about objective improvements in policies or outcomes or about widespread recognition of success.

In evaluating the utility of irrationality, Simon opens a can of worms by raising a question about the value limitations of the concept:

> We can see that reason is wholly instrumental. It cannot tell us where to go; at best it can tell us how to get there. It is a gun for hire that can be employed in the service of whatever goals we have, good or bad. It makes a great difference in

our view of the human condition whether we attribute our difficulties to evil or to ignorance and irrationality—to the baseness of our goals or to not knowing how to reach them.[64]

Others[65] contend that reason can be necessary to develop and use both values and priorities, while sufficient for neither. This controversy about the relationship between irrationality and values shows the confusion about whether preferring irrationality should be based on evaluation of means alone or ends as well.

The claim that intended and unintended irrationality can be beneficial in international relations is unusual but by no means unique. Most foreign policy analysts do agree that "irrational processes are presumably less likely to lead to accurate perceptions and effective policies than are rational ones,"[66] and that rationality enables us to solve our problems and may even be essential for our survival.[67] However, at least some general arguments, to be presented in chapter seven, exist in the literature about the positive effects of irrationality (or the negative effects of rationality).

Ultimately, of course, the reader will develop particular notions about the nature, sources, perceptions, and utility of irrationality through this book, and these notions may very well not correspond to those of the author. But in order to clarify further the assumptions behind this study, the next chapter provides a detailed discussion of the methodology used in choosing and analyzing the case studies

2.

Methodology for Case Study Analysis

This book chooses the "focused comparison" case study approach as the means of examining the consequences of irrationality in international confrontations. Though casually used for decades, this focused comparison method was only recently formalized and systematized by George and Smoke.[1] This approach examines multiple cases and draws its conclusions by making comparisons among them with respect to a prespecified set of investigative areas. Differences as well as similarities emerge from this kind of analysis, with the result being carefully conditionalized generalizations about patterns. The technique sacrifices the high reliability of statistical analysis of aggregate data for greater policy relevance and more comprehensive coverage of hard-to-measure variables.

This last advantage is particularly essential for the study of irrationality. As the previous chapter's theoretical discussion indicates, the concept involves such subjective, mercurial, intangible, and context-relative aspects that it would be quite difficult to quantify or break down into observable components. To make the assessments needed for statistical analysis would seem to invalidate much of the data because of the untested assumptions and leaps of logic necessitated. At the same time, empirically exploring irrationality simply through a single case study or anecdotal references to historical case studies, as is too often characteristic of psychological studies in international relations, would provide little basis for sound generalization or meaningful policy prescription. So the focused comparison approach provides a useful methodological compromise.

HISTORICAL AND GEOGRAPHICAL BASIS FOR CASE SELECTION

The sample of twelve cases selected for analysis is designed to be representative of very recent manifestations of irrationality in international confrontations. All of the cases occurred in the 1980's, providing a relatively homogeneous international context as a backdrop. Analyzing confrontations which occurred so recently reduces the availability of broad and detached historical perspective, but at the same time increases the relevance of the evaluation to current policy making. Many of the incidents chosen have never been part of a comparative investigation, and a few have not been the subject of systematic scrutiny even in isolation. Furthermore, exploring post–1980 cases avoids dwelling on certain incidents—such as the Cuban Missile Crisis, Pearl Harbor, and Vietnam—which have been beseiged by foreign policy analysis almost to the point of overkill.

Geographically, the goal is to provide balanced global coverage. Most cases usually studied deal directly or indirectly with American foreign policy, and this sample consciously attempts to avoid that somewhat ethnocentric focus. The regional distribution of the locations in which the cases occurred is as follows: two in East Asia, two in Africa, two in Western Europe, one in Eastern Europe, two in Central America, and one in South America. In each case, this study identifies an initiator, not to point a finger at which nation is responsible for beginning the confrontation but rather to highlight which state launched the particular decisions or actions classified and evaluated as irrational. Fewer than half of the cases involve superpower initiators, and only two involve superpower targets. Half of the initiators and two-thirds of the targets are nations which are not even great powers.

CASE GOALS, STRATEGIES, IRRATIONALITY, AND OUTCOMES

The focused comparison of cases encompasses a brief summary or the background of the confrontation, the goals identified by and/or attributed to the irrational state, the strategies it consciously or unconsciously chooses to attain these goals, the nature of the irrationality involved, and the outcome of the use of irrationality. In the means-ends analysis, there is explicit sensitivity to the possibilities of amorphous and poorly defined goals and strategies, conflicting goals and strategies, and goals and strategies that change over time in the course of the confrontation.

Half of the selected cases involve stick-in-the-mud irrationality and half daredevil irrationality. The vast majority of the cases display more than one dimension of irrationality, and so there is adequate representation of incompatibility with goals, consensus, or outcomes, noncomprehensive search-and-evaluation, inconsistency of statements and/or actions, and non-dispassionate style of decision. Irrationality also occurs during more than one phase of each case, although it is often difficult to pinpoint exactly the beginning and ending. This study does not claim that the selected cases are those which displayed the greatest irrationality in the early 1980's, but rather only that they manifest significant irrationality. There is certain to be disagreement about whether, when, and how irrationality was present in each case. Clearly a state's belief that some other state is acting irrationally is neither a necessary nor a sufficient prerequisite for classifying behavior as irrational. In most of the cases, it is unclear whether the irrationality is intended or unintended, whether it is a conscious ruse or a sincere reflection of the decision-making process.

Concerning the outcome of the use of irrationality—whether or not a country succeeds or fails in achieving its goals—half of the selected cases seem largely successes and half largely failures. As with other judgments here, assessing the outcome of irrationality in a given confrontation proves to be controversial both in terms of whether the outcome is successful and whether the outcome is in any way a result of the irrationality involved in the confrontation (as opposed to the variety of other determinants of success and failure). Deciding a confrontation's outcome depends heavily on debatable determinations of which states are chosen as initiator and target, what time period during the confrontation is selected for analysis, and how the irrational state's goals are identified. Moreover, evaluating outcomes of confrontations which are still ongoing is particularly tentative. Nonetheless, this study tries to marshal the evidence fairly and to identify explicitly weak links in the assessments.

Table 1 displays in chronological order the list of cases studied, the dates of each confrontation, and the identities of the initiator and target in each case. The first two cases, focusing on Kampuchea and Namibia, had occurred for years before 1980, but the case analyses examine the irrationality present only in the post–1980 period. One-third of the cases were still ongoing and unresolved when the research was completed in Spring 1985.

SOURCE MATERIALS AND LIMITS TO GENERALIZATION

Because the included cases are so recent and irrationality is so difficult to document, relevant primary sources of information are generally not available. As a result, secondary sources comprise the bulk of the data base. Fortunately, due to the prominence of most of the cases, these secondary sources are usually high quality and provide adequate insight into the role of irrationality in the confrontations. The interpretation of each case always relies on numerous sources of various ideological slants. While the accuracy of some of the source materials is not flawless, particularly for ongoing incidents, the reliability of these materials seems unexpectedly high.

Given the research design, sampling scheme, and data base specified, the findings which emerge have limited generalizability. Extrapolation of results—either across time to different historical periods, across space to nations not covered, or across types of interaction to routine nonconfrontational incidents—can be done only with great caution due to the small number of cases considered and the frailty of the data base. Furthermore, combining findings derived specifically for particular facets of irrationality appear to

Table 1
Case Studies of International Confrontation

Case	Dates	Initiator	Target
Struggle for Kampuchea	1980-present	China	Vietnam
Namibia Sovereignty Dispute	1980-present	South Africa	Namibia
Iranian Seizure of American Hostages	November 1979-January 1981	Iran	US
Poland Solidarity Crisis	July 1980-December 1982	USSR	Poland
Iran-Iraq War	September 1980-present	Iraq	Iran
Soviet Natural Gas Pipeline Controversy	December 1981-November 1982	US	USSR
American Harassment of Nicaragua	March 1982-present	US	Nicaragua
Falkland Islands War	April 1982-June 1982	Argentina	UK
Somali Territorial Dispute	June 1982-present	Somalia	Ethiopia
Korean Airlines Incident	September 1983	USSR	South Korea
Grenada Invasion	October 1983-December 1983	US	Grenada
Libyan Embassy Incident	April 1984	Libya	UK

be inadvisable, for substantial differences exist among them. The policy implications at the end of the book are thus presented with considerable tentativeness.

This discussion of methodology sets the stage for the presentation of the case studies in the next four chapters. While the restrictions on validity, reliability, and generalizability are great, they in no way detract from the fascinating and sometimes startling revelations of irrationality in the confrontations which follow.

3.

"Stick-in-the-Mud" Irrationality—Successes

The first set of case studies examined are those which exhibit stick-in-the-mud irrationality and have relatively successful outcomes. The specific confrontations chosen are China's struggle with Vietnam over the status of Kampuchea, South Africa's attempt to maintain control over Namibia, and the Soviet Union's machinations during the Solidarity crisis in Poland. Each is a regional confrontation involving efforts by the initiator to maintain some control over an area deemed to be within its sphere of influence.

THE STRUGGLE FOR KAMPUCHEA

Kampuchea (or, more traditionally, Cambodia) is one of the oldest Southeast Asian states, with a recorded history dating back to the seventh century.[1] There have been long-standing territorial disputes between Vietnam and Kampuchea over the delta regions of southern Vietnam formerly belonging to Kampuchea and over a number of islands in the Gulf of Thailand.

Most analysts agree that "few nations in history have experienced the cumulative disasters and destruction which have engulfed Cambodia during the past two decades."[2] During the Vietnam War of the 1960's and 1970's, North Vietnam used Kampuchea as a staging ground for fighting South Vietnam, and after a bloody battle the communist Khmer Rouge took over the Kampuchean government and installed the regime of President Khieu Sampan and Premier

Pol Pot. The net result was the destruction of the Kampuchean economy and the creation of a massive refugee problem. After the end of the Vietnam War in 1975, the Khmer Rouge "tried to destroy a culture which had endured for more than a millenium," and at least a million Kampucheans lost their lives through murder and starvation during the three and one-half years of Khmer Rouge rule.[3]

Vietnam initially sponsored and supported the Khmer Rouge in order "to control the Cambodian communists as thoroughly as it controlled those in South Vietnam and Laos."[4] After all, Vietnam had provided the opening for the Khmer Rouge's seizure of power in Kampuchea when, in 1970, the Vietnamese army decimated the Kampuchean army. In 1978, "having failed to dominate and control the Khmer Rouge, Hanoi decided to depose them and replace them with a more pliable communist regime."[5] On December 25th of that year Vietnam, buoyed by the signing of the Peace and Friendship Treaty with the Soviet Union in early November and anxious to exert its hegemony in Indochina, militarily invaded Kampuchea, deposed the infamous Pol Pot regime, and installed a puppet government (the People's Republic of Kampuchea) under Heng Samrin, Pol Pot's former lieutenant.

China refused to accept the change in the balance of power in the region[6] and launched a counter-attack against Vietnam in February 1979. From that point until the present, China has been actively fueling a guerrilla war against the Vietnam-controlled regime in Kampuchea. While the China-backed guerrilla force seems unlikely to gain outright victory against the Vietnamese troops, it does seem to be fully capable of prolonged resistance (in the manner of Vietnamese guerrillas fighting American troops in the earlier war), thus keeping Kampuchea in turmoil.

Of the 200,000 Vietnamese troops involved in the invasion in 1978–79, by late 1983 there were about 150,000 left occupying Kampuchea, augmenting the 20,000 to 30,000 troops of the puppet Samrin government there.[7] Vietnam's claim that it remains in Kampuchea only to prevent Pol Pot's return to power seems to be a "thinly disguised deception,"[8] and indeed Vietnam has stated that it will withdraw its forces only when the "Chinese threat" ends and Sino-Vietnamese differences are resolved:[9] these differences include not only the Kampuchean dispute but also disputed islands in the South China Sea, Sino-Vietnamese boundary issues, and reparations for China's invasion of Vietnam. In sustaining this occupation and pressing these demands, Vietnam is actively supported by the Soviet Union, which gives more than two billion dollars a year in military and economic aid to Vietnam.[10] The long-term expectations involved in the Vietnamese occupation of Kampuchea are vividly demonstrated by the over 50,000 Vietnamese nationals who have been resettled in Kampuchea since 1980.[11]

The anti-Vietnamese guerrilla forces in Kampuchea are organized into an uneasy alliance called the Coalition Government of Democratic Kampuchea, made up of three groups:[12] the National Army of Democratic Kampuchea, nominally headed by the Khmer Rouge's Pol Pot and consisting of about 50,000 soldiers; the Kampuchean People's National Liberation Front, headed by former Kampuchean premier Son Sann and consisting of about 12,000 soldiers; and the Moulinaka, headed by former Kampuchean president Norodom Sihanouk and consisting of about 2,500 soldiers. As Van der Kroef points out,[13] "There is little love lost between these coalition partners," and "the armed followings of each leader have retained separate organizational identities and military independence." China supplies the coalition with substantial quantities of weapons, ammunition, and fuel.

The Association of Southeast Asian Nations (ASEAN) has assumed the "leading role" in the search "for a solution to the Cambodian crisis that can restore stability to the region and end the suffering of the Khmer people."[14] The United Nations has also been quite concerned with this dispute, and in July 1981 a UN-sponsored International Conference on Kampuchea recommended a cease-fire and the holding of free elections under UN supervision. Vietnam has consistently rejected UN and ASEAN initiatives on this issue, and has consequently become diplomatically isolated; a severe slap-in-the-face occurred on October 20, 1983 when the UN General Assembly approved the seating of the Coalition Government of Democratic Kampuchea as the legitimate ruling authority of the nation.

China's Goals and Strategies

The cornerstone of China's policy toward Kampuchea in this struggle has been supporting Kampuchea as a "separate, independent entity."[15] China's militant moves in Kampuchea have been motivated by a desire not only to contain Vietnamese expansionism but also to meet the more serious Soviet challenge posed by this expansion.[16] Indeed, the Soviet involvement has seemed to transform "a localized border war" into "a contest between China and the Soviet Union for pre-eminence in Indochina."[17]

After a Vietnamese troop withdrawal, China appears willing to accept the results of free elections in Kampuchea. On March 1, 1983 the PRC Ministry of Foreign Affairs issued a five-point plan for dealing with Kampuchea, and the last point states that "China is willing to refrain from any interference in the internal affairs of Kampuchea, to respect the independence, neutrality, and non-aligned status of Kampuchea, and to respect the result of the Kampuchean people's choice made through a genuinely free election to be held under U.N. supervision."[18] Admittedly, the specific nature of the neutrality and non-aligned status was left ambiguous,[19] but China does not appear to seek ultimate control of Kampuchea: "Throughout the alliance, Beijing by and large played the role of a benevolent bigger brother and never assumed a dominating posture in its dealing with Kampuchea."[20]

In recent years China has felt that support for guerrilla resistance was the best strategy "to deprive the Vietnamese of any legitimacy for their stay in Kampuchea, to act as a focus of Kampuchean nationalism, and to increase the costs to Vietnam for its occupation."[21] There are elaborate underpinnings to this strategy:

> Although China does not expect to achieve a miracle by suddenly turning the tide of war in Kampuchea, it is at least prepared to wear Vietnam down through a protracted guerrilla war. By continuing to bleed the Vietnamese for as long as possible, China presumably hopes to make the Vietnamese occupation militarily so costly as to render it politically untenable, thereby ushering in a change either in Hanoi's basic policy toward Kampuchea or in its leadership structure which would eventually also bring about policy reorientation. At the same time, by maintaining the credibility of the anti-Vietnamese resistance movement and expanding its political and operational bases as much as possible, China also seeks as an immediate aim to ensure that the military situation in Kam-

puchea will not become so unfavourable as to lend any cre-
dence to the legitimacy of the Heng Samrin regime.[22]

Unless Vietnam withdraws, China seems committed to the "let's
bleed Vietnam white" tactic through protracted struggle.[23]

China's Irrationality

China's policy in the struggle for Kampuchea displays significant
stick-in-the-mud irrationality. Barring Vietnamese withdrawal,
China plans to continue indefinitely supporting the anti-government
guerrillas, a position well described by one analyst as "implaca-
ble."[24] The PRC appears to be distinctly underreactive, in terms of
changing its policies to cope with fluctuating Vietnamese actions in
Kampuchea. Mahbubani[25] sums up well this stagnant policy: "Unlike the French or the Americans, the Chinese are never going to
withdraw from the border or the region. . . . One Chinese leader is
reported to have remarked [that] the Vietnamese have picked up a
huge boulder and dropped it on their own feet." China intransi-
gently considers its policy of containing Vietnam as "a matter of
principle not to be negotiated or changed."[26]

Of the specific dimensions of irrationality, China has displayed
most graphically a non-dispassionate style of decision. The PRC's
rhetoric on this issue has been extraordinarily emotional, reflecting
the intensity of its feelings. Chang[27] stresses "the bitter and strongly
didactic tone" of China's accusations of Vietnam and Chinese desires "to penalize Vietnam for its willfulness and arrogance"; the
"vehement" nature of Chinese charges of Soviet-Vietnamese collusion in pursuit of hegemony; the "deliberately hostile" nature of
China's Vietnam policy; the "belligerent" position China has taken
on the territorial dispute and the ethnic crisis involved; and the
vengeful Chinese view that there is still a need for "administering
lessons to Vietnam." Furthermore, Vietnam has assumed that China's emotional and material support for Kampuchea has been the
root cause behind Kampuchea's willingness to turn against Vietnam
so violently and with such intense hostility, and that China has thus
fanned the flames of the Khmer Rouge's "revolutionary fanati-

cism."[28] This emotionalism has been present not just in China's pronouncements but in its decision-making process as well: the Chinese feel they have been "driven beyond their forbearance" through escalating "Vietnamese provocations and harassment."[29]

Outcome of Irrationality Use

Up until a massive Vietnamese offensive against Kampuchea begun in late 1984, the overwhelming assessment of the prevailing situation was long-term stalemate.[30] Most have agreed that "China's plan seems to be working":[31] "Hanoi has failed to fully occupy some areas along Kampuchea's border with Thailand—the main staging base for the insurgent armies"; "the entire northern sector is said by Western intelligence sources to be vulnerable to guerrilla attack"; and "the end of the war is nowhere in sight." Vietnam "continues to suffer humiliating defeats over the Kampuchean issue on the world stage" and is in a perilously stagnant economic situation, "cut off from the world money markets and sources of development capital and technical assistance."[32] While clearly not eliminating Vietnamese control of Kampuchea, China's stick-in-the-mud strategy appears to have prevented the degree of control Vietnam desires and to have raised the costs of attempting to maintain what control exists. Even after Vietnam's notable victory in its dry season offensive against Kampuchea in 1984–85, the costs of control remain high: "While Vietnam may have won the border war, it is faced with formidable difficulties in occupying Kampuchea."[33] Although no incontrovertible link can be established between China's non-dispassionate style and this outcome, at least one account ties Vietnamese awareness of Chinese wrath to Vietnam's "relatively frantic efforts" to get Sino-Vietnamese talks going.[34]

THE NAMIBIA SOVEREIGNTY DISPUTE

After Germany established the colony of South West Africa in the 1880's, South Africa captured the territory in 1915, and in 1920 the League of Nations gave South Africa a mandate to govern the territory. South Africa pursued a policy of land deprivation and segregation at that time, broadening the scope of discrimination beyond what the Germans had practiced. At the end of World War II, South Africa asked the United Nations for permission to incorporate the territory, and upon denial refused to accept a United Nations trusteeship agreement for Namibia. Until 1966, Namibia technically remained a mandate, but the South African government did not submit reports on its administration, and so the UN periodically censured South Africa. In 1966, the United Nations declared the mandate terminated and placed the territory under UN control, but South Africa refused to comply. In subsequent years the UN has passed a number of resolutions declaring South Africa's continued occupation of Namibia as illegal. In 1978, South Africa agreed in principle to UN Security Council Resolution 435, which describes a compromise settlement leading eventually to Namibia's independence, but no significant change has occurred as a result.

There are many parties to this sovereignty dispute aside from South Africa and the United Nations. The "contact group" of five Western nations—Canada, France, the United Kingdom, the United States, and West Germany—has been working since 1977 with the UN in direct negotiation with South Africa. This group has attempted to achieve a settlement which would both recognize Namibian human rights and protect Western interests in South Africa, a two-pronged effort that some[35] see as inherently contradictory. SWAPO—the South-West African People's Organization—was founded in 1960 and is the only significant national liberation movement in Namibia.[36] Since 1965 its militant faction has waged a guerrilla war against South Africa's occupying forces, and in February 1983 SWAPO launched a series of particularly punishing attacks against the South African army. South Africa has detained, imprisoned, or exiled many of SWAPO's leaders because of the security threat posed by SWAPO's alleged links to outside communist agitators. DTA (Democratic Turnhalle Alliance) was established in 1977 and represents the conservative voice of whites and other non-black ethnic groups in Namibia. DTA's interests are to bring Namibia independence under the protective umbrella of South Africa. Although other political organizations exist inside Namibia, such as the South-West Africa branch of South Africa's pro-apartheid National Party and the Namibia National Front, SWAPO and DTA have traditionally been the principal internal antagonists. A new relevant actor emerged when Cuban troops entered Angola in 1975, for South Africa then asserted that it would not leave Namibia before the Cubans left Angola.[37] This last development has caused the dispute to connect more directly to the Cold War, although the issue has somewhat faded since the Lusaka agreement in February 1984, in which South Africa agreed to disengage its forces from southern Angola and the two nations established a Joint Monitoring Commission to oversee the withdrawal.

Namibia possesses a number of characteristics which give it special strategic importance. Economically, the Western powers control the major corporations there, and Namibia makes a significant contribution to South African revenue.[38] Namibia is the world's sixth largest source of diamonds and the world's fourth largest source of uranium, and is a major exporter of copper as well. South Africa has invested a considerable amount of it own capital in Namibia. The port at Walvis Bay is crucial for geopolitical reasons, and South Africa views Namibia as a buffer against the neighboring hostile black African states. For these states, Namibia is a critical symbol of the extension of degrading South African racist policies.[39] All of these concerns make Namibia, as South Africa terms it, a "plum worth the fight."[40]

South Africa's Goals and Strategies

South Africa's ideal long-term goal in Namibia is the achievement of a semi-independent Namibia—safely managed from South Africa, without a SWAPO government, and with full international recognition.[41] The short-term goal of South Africa has been "defeating the internal SWAPO insurgents along with containing the Angolans, Cubans, and Russians to the north."[42] While only a few analysts contend that South Africa believes that it can "stay in Namibia indefinitely,"[43] South Africa is heavily constrained by conservative domestic opinion, including the National Party parliamentary caucus, which holds the government accountable for preventing the establishment of a hostile Namibian regime.[44] As Seiler[45] astutely points out, "only if the U.S. government provided an unequivocal guarantee to South Africa of security against conventional military attack—an improbable commitment even for the

Reagan Administration, given the domestic political repercussions of such an act—then South Africa might acquiesce to a Namibian election won by SWAPO."

There is internal disagreement within South Africa about the best strategies to achieve these goals and about the extent to which South Africa needs to satisfy the Western contact group.[46] Currently South Africa has a multifaceted strategy: "Pretoria believes its present approach—combining military intervention, covert aid to sympathetic anti-black-regime organisations, economic coercion, with economic and political support for trusted friends—can be the basis for stable and productive regional relationships."[47] South Africa may have even "decided to use its military and economic strength to bludgeon its neighbours into adopting a more pliant attitude," in which a new "fortress South Africa" prepares "to withstand the 'total onslaught' supposedly being directed against it from the Soviet Union."[48] However, as Donald McHenry (former American ambassador to the UN) notes, the basic underlying tactic seems to be one of stalling:

> Thus, the South Africans went into a stall that is still going on and is likely to last. There were all kinds of ways to stall. Accuse the United Nations or Donald McHenry or any number of other groups of unfairness. Talk endlessly about the military contingents of the United Nations. Have a long discussion about where the UN forces were to be stationed, what kind of uniforms they would wear, whether or not they would have commissary rights, and whether these included hard liquor. Such disputes over details of implementation went on and on.[49]

Although making time through military occupation is expensive, South Africa perceives it to be the best way of "postponing a political solution while trying to rearrange the balance of forces in the region in order to usher in a pliant regime."[50]

South Africa's Irrationality

It is probably evident from the preceding analysis that South African policy toward Namibia displays stick-in-the-mud irrationality. While some[51] try to project a rational responsiveness to this policy—"it is logical to let go, and since the South Africans are rational, they will let go"—this assumption does not seem to conform to reality. The previously described stalling strategy is a classic underreactive, stick-in-the-mud tactic. As Rotberg[52] bluntly states, "South Africans have never wanted the negotiations to succeed." Seiler provides the best example of this refusal to modify a cautious, sluggish, and stagnant foreign policy toward Namibia despite major changes in external circumstances:

> Robert Mugabe's massive electoral win in Zimbabwe during January 1980 also marked a critical turning point for Namibia—at least, everyone but Pretoria thought so. With widespread confidence that the South Africans would come to the 'right' conclusion—that their interests demanded a rapid resolution in Namibia in order to limit the impact of a certain SWAPO victory—the contact group, the front-line states, SWAPO, and the U.N. Secretariat agreed that South Africa should be given a brief period of time to digest the election results. But no discernible urgency was shown in Pretoria.[53]

South Africa never did react with important moves to this or many other significant recent developments in the Namibian situation.

Two dimensions of irrationality emerge in this case: non-comprehensive search-and-evaluation and inconsistency of statements and/or actions. Turning to the first dimension, South Africa has incompletely and inadequately analyzed the realities of the Namibia dispute: "Pretoria persists with administrative and military policies based on profoundly incorrect perceptions about Namibian blacks, about SWAPO, and about the overall state of regional political relationships."[54] More specifically, South Africa maintains an overly optimistic view of the situation, perhaps reflecting wishful thinking. South Africa has ignored "the disintegrative impact of its involvement on existent social and community ties" in Namibia; overlooked the failure of DTA to provide a political alternative to SWAPO acceptable to the majority of blacks; and underestimated "the depth of African commitment to genuine black governance in Namibia in its preemptive raids and acts of economic coercion and reprisal, which assume that its regional neighbours will acquiesce in South African political preferences if enough pressure is applied on them."[55]

As to inconsistency of statements and/or actions, South Africa has made this an almost constant feature of its dealing with pressure from the UN and the Western contact group. Shepherd[56] notes that "South African leaders have skillfully utilized this Western interest and manipulated the conflict to appear to be accepting reform, in favor of rights, while preserving the dependence of Namibia and its tributary role." Repeatedly South Africa has given lip service to timetables leading to Namibian independence, and then has never followed through with action.[57] One analyst[58] characterizes South Africa as "playing games" in Namibia: in July 1983, for example, while the United States was negotiating for a Cuban troop withdrawal from Angola as a means of facilitating Namibian independence, South Africa implemented a new constitution for the territory despite claiming noninterference in the negotiations. The explanation was either that South Africa did "not share the American State Department's optimism" that an agreement with the Cubans was imminent, or that South Africa intended "to find some new pretext for stalling should an agreement be reached."[59]

Outcome of Irrationality Use

While South Africa certainly has not been effective in achieving all of its objectives, it has succeeded at least up to this point in its primary short-term goal of preventing a hostile regime from taking power in Namibia. International negotiations over Namibia have generally reached an impasse. Without South African intervention, SWAPO would in all probability now be ruling Namibia. The South African military has successfully destroyed the military part of SWAPO and has been encountering increasingly favorable plans for settlement of the dispute from the Western contact group.[60] South Africa has even conducted effective punitive measures against neighboring Angola and Zambia for their support of SWAPO.[61] Despite the regional and global unpopularity of its views, South Africa has managed to place itself in "the driver's seat" in the Namibian sovereignty dispute—"negotiations will succeed only when South Africa wants them to succeed."[62] While a considerable part of the credit has to go to tacit Western support for South Africa, the stick-in-the-mud, myopic, and duplicitous policy has also played a key role.

THE POLAND SOLIDARITY CRISIS

The Polish workers' crisis began on July 1, 1980 when the Polish government drastically raised meat prices, triggering an immediate series of work stoppages and strikes by Polish working people. This crisis had resulted from the failure of the economic policies of Polish First Secretary Edward Gierek. Gierek had become head of state in 1970 and had introduced a "new development strategy" relying heavily on large infusions of Western technology and on Western financing, but this strategy encountered mounting difficulties since the mid–1970's.[63] These difficulties revolved around the rising price of oil, the European recession, unrealistic investment policies, bad harvests, and the absence of meaningful economic reforms. By the late 1970's the situation had become so dire that "it had become evident, not only to the Polish working class but to the population as a whole, that Poland faced nothing less than the collapse of its planning and management system and the total bankruptcy of its economy."[64] The accompanying trend of the government's greater ideological and political orthodoxy helped to create tensions with both the intellectuals and the Church, especially by 1980 when the Polish economy suffered from skyrocketing inflation, foreign debt, and declining national income.[65]

By mid-August 1980 the spreading labor disturbances in Poland were more organized and later that month representatives of twenty-one enterprises from the Gdansk area formed the Inter-Factory Strike Committee. On August 22nd the committee presented to the Polish government a series of political and economic demands, including the acceptance of free trade unions. On August 31, 1980 a government commission officially granted the workers' committee significant concessions: the right to strike, reduction in censorship, increases in wages, improvement in working conditions, abolition of party privileges, and a five-day work week. The Polish workers, "well aware that their strength lies in concerted action,"[66] symbolically called their new national union "Solidarity," and it soon officially registered as an "independent, self-governing labor union." Lech Walesa, a shipyard worker in Gdansk, quickly emerged as Solidarity's leader.

The results of this agreement were far-reaching. On September 6, 1980 Stanislaw Kania replaced Gierek, and the new Polish leadership consisted "basically of politically conservative communists who at the same time acknowledged the need for reforms, particularly in the areas of the economy and the relationship between Party and workers."[67] Thousands of members of the Polish Communist Party resigned or were purged, and close to a million others joined Solidarity. The students, the Church, and even ethnic minorities became increasingly vocal in anti-government, pro-Solidarity activities. The involvement of all of these diverse Polish interests among the masses of the general population, rather than narrow state or party interests, is the primary explanation of Solidarity's success.[68] The Soviet Union, clearly unhappy with the chaotic state of affairs, condemned the "subversive" and "counterrevolutionary" forces in Poland which had created "anarchy and disorder," and began in 1980–81 holding large Warsaw Pact military maneuvers in and around Poland.

On September 9–10, 1981 Solidarity extended its demands by calling for free elections to the Parliament, the formation of free trade unions by other East European nations, and greater self-management by Polish workers. On October 18, 1981 General Wojciech Jaruzelski replaced Kania as head of state and immediately adopted a hardline policy toward Solidarity, which continued to gain strength and publicity for its demands. Finally, on December 13, 1981, Jaruzelski imposed martial law and suspended the reforms which Solidarity had achieved. Solidarity was taken by surprise, and Lech Walesa and its other leaders were imprisoned. Western Europe responded with indignation to the repression in Poland, and the United States instituted economic sanctions against both Poland and the Soviet Union, including those affecting the Soviet natural gas pipeline (discussed in chapter four). Gradually the tension lowered, and on December 31, 1982 Poland suspended its martial law. But Solidarity and the independent labor movement have been outlawed since October 8, 1982, although Walesa still meets with underground Solidarity leaders to make plans for continuing the struggle against the Polish government.

Soviet Union's Goals and Strategies

The primary Soviet goal in the Poland Solidarity crisis was "to pressure the Polish leadership into taking a firmer line toward Solidarity and halting the process of inner erosion that has beset the party since August 1980."[69] Several analysts[70] considered the Polish crisis to be the most profound threat to Soviet domination of Eastern Europe in the postwar period, because earlier challenges were "revolutions from above" led by dissident intellectuals and disaffected party members, while the Polish situation represented a broad-based "revolution from below" led by workers. Poland is critical to the Soviet Union as a buffer against Western Europe, a major source of soldiers for the Warsaw Pact, and a producer of needed goods for the communist bloc. The Soviets were justifiably concerned about the spread of the workers' revolt to other Eastern European states: "As the Kremlin realizes, the stability of Soviet domination of Eastern Europe depends on the relative docility of the Eastern European countries. To the extent that the 'Polish disease' may grow in strength, it may also grow more contagious and infect Poland's neighbors—the Soviet Union included."[71]

The strategies used by the Soviet Union to pursue the objective of containing and de-escalating the Polish crisis were mainly conducting Warsaw Pact military maneuvers in and around Poland and overtly and covertly pressuring the Polish Communist Party and Polish officials to quell the disturbance. Specifically, the Soviets upgraded the readiness of their troops in the western military districts, extended the "Soyuz 81" military maneuvers, and even openly criticized the Polish government on occasion.[72] In the Soviet Union's attempt "to strengthen the intestinal fortitude of the Polish party leaders,"[73] it went so far as to orchestrate directly and indirectly the changes of leadership in Poland.

Soviet Union's Irrationality

Despite some fluctuation in the intensity of Soviet actions toward Poland during the crisis, the USSR basically followed a policy characterized by stick-in-the-mud irrationality—placing continued, but often subtle, pressure on the Polish government to deal with the worker problem. Regardless of changes in circumstances, such as West European disapproval and American sanctions, this course of action remained unchanged, and the determination to see the problem through to its resolution continued unabated. The Soviet Union utilized an approach of "waiting patiently"—while applying necessary prods—for circumstances to evolve in a more favorable direction (such as for the 800,000 lost members of the Polish Communist Party to return to the fold).[74] Laqueur perhaps best describes this long-term dialectic Soviet approach in the latter stages of the Polish crisis:

> Closer to home, the Soviets had to deal with the Polish problem. Their tactic was to avoid dealing with it—allowing General Wojciech Jaruzelski to muddle through with occasional gestures of approval from Moscow, and occasional hints to crack down harder. In general the Soviets appeared to have calculated that the rest of Europe would accommodate to the new Polish regime, despite its odious behavior.[75]

The Soviet policy seemed to be to wear down internal and external opposition through perseverance and patience.

The Soviet Union appears to have exhibited three dimensions of irrationality during the Polish crisis—inconsistency of statements and/or actions, non-comprehensive search-and-evaluation, and incompatibility of decisions with goals, consensus, or outcomes. The first dimension, involving inconsistency, occurred at two levels. First, the Soviet Union claimed at various times in the crisis that its role was simply supporting the Polish government and not directly interfering in Poland's internal affairs, but this claim was contradicted by the aforementioned Soviet manipulation of Polish leadership and the absence of any "evidence to suggest that the

Soviet Politburo ever considered allowing events in Poland to take their own course."[76] Second, there was an inconsistency between Soviet military signals and the political solution undertaken in Poland: the Soviet Union underwent the costly preparatory process for military intervention in Poland in December 1980 and March 1981 and may have seriously entertained actually intervening in both cases;[77] the subsequent absence of military intervention may have sent contradictory messages to relevant parties.

The second and third dimensions of irrationality, non-comprehensive search-and-evaluation and incompatibility of the decision process with goals, reflect considerable differences within the Soviet Politburo on how to deal with the Polish crisis.[78] But the considerations governing these differences seemed not to focus on the overall impact on Soviet national interests: "In deciding what to do in Poland, the political leaders of the USSR were guided more by personal calculations about their own particular interests—that is, by power relationships within the Politburo—than by considerations of international repercussions arising from their actions."[79] Thus a tradeoff appeared to exist between the quality of the decisions—how well they served the overall goals of the Soviet Union—and the acceptability of the decisions—how well they conformed to the self-interest-oriented consensus in the Politburo. Anderson more precisely specifies the kind of unsystematic calculation involved in decisions about Poland:

> In sum, it would appear that in Soviet decision-making the benefits of a policy to the Politburo as a whole are less important than the advantages or disadvantages it brings to individual members. Moreover, the individuals tend to make up their mind on policy issues largely on the basis of personal calculations. While each of them must take into account the need to maintain the power of the Politburo as a whole, policy issues capable of significantly affecting the Politburo's collective standing must be rare. Furthermore, the collective interest is only one element, and apparently not the key one, in the calculations of individual members.[80]

To distort their assessment of issues for these personal ambitions, Soviet decision makers seem to "exaggerate the benefits and minimize the costs of policies they favor, and give a reverse twist to policies they oppose."[81] Thus bureaucratic politics distortion, impeding sound analysis of policy issues, was alive and well in the Soviet Union during the Poland crisis.

Outcome of Irrationality Use

Despite the continued existence of Solidarity and of low-level turmoil in Poland, the Soviet Union has been largely successful in its goals there. Jaruzelski's imposition of martial law produced a quieting of the Polish workers' visible opposition to government policies and "accomplished the objective that the Soviet Union had in mind since the late summer of 1980."[82] Furthermore, the international indignation has since died down:[83] "Legitimacy seemed to be conferred by the visit of the Pope [in summer 1983], which the regime handled without major incident"; and "a gradual easing of sanctions and a relief from debt payments also suggested the West was accepting Jaruzelski." The Soviet Union's unwavering, persistent pressure appears to have played a major role both in reducing the disturbances in Poland and in increasing international acceptance of the new status quo there.

SYNTHESIS

In each of these three cases, the nation in question used a largely deterrent strategy to pursue a status quo goal of maintenance of sphere of influence: China attempted through support of guerrillas to prevent Vietnamese control of Kampuchea; South Africa attempted through stalling to prevent the independence of Namibia (or its control by antagonistic forces); and the Soviet Union attempted through subtle pressures to prevent the liberalization movement in Poland from going too far. When one state endeavors to prevent change in another, particularly if the target state is proximate or has a history of being dominated by the initiating state, it appears that stick-in-the-mud irrationality can be quite effective. The reasons behind this effectiveness (repugnant as it may sound to some) seem to involve the combination of the initiator's immense power advantage with a persistent stance which is credible due to recent regional demonstrations of power.

This type of irrationality seems to work best as a deterrent strategy when the threat to upset the status quo has origins largely internal to the target state, as in the case of the internal labor movement in Poland; fairly well when the threat involves a mix of internal and external origins, as in the case of SWAPO and Cuba in Namibia; and least well when the threat has largely external origins, as in the case of the Vietnamese in Kampuchea. This pattern results from the more direct experience, in comparison to any non-satellite nation, which a satellite has in being subjected to the coercive power of the dominating state; the more the turmoil emerges from within the satellite rather than from outside agitation, the more the stick-in-the-mud approach can reap the benefits of past coercive experience.

In a related manner, stick-in-the-mud irrationality appears to be most effective for deterrent purposes when the initiating state only threatens the direct use of military force to achieve its objectives, as in the Poland case, rather than actually employing such force, as in the Kampuchea and Namibia cases. Because of the initiating state's previously discussed power advantage and history of domination over the target, there seems to be no inherent need to utilize military force to convince the target state of resolve or credibility of threat. Indeed, involvement in direct military combat could embroil the initiator in an unproductive conflict or cause it to stray beyond its status quo objectives, thereby reducing the legitimacy of its actions. Because stick-in-the-mud irrationality depends on long-term persistence, short-term costs and risks need to be minimized.

4.

"Stick-in-the-Mud" Irrationality—Failures

The second set of case studies also exhibit stick-in-the-mud irrationality but were unsuccessful, failing to achieve key objectives. The confrontations included are the American involvement in the Soviet natural gas pipeline controversy, the American harassment of Nicaragua, and Somalia's conflict with Ethiopia. Each case involves an attempt by the initiator to reverse an unpleasant predicament confronting it.

THE SOVIET NATURAL GAS PIPELINE CONTROVERSY

Construction of the Soviet natural gas pipeline began only after considerable planning and negotiations. The pipeline is designed to run 2,800 miles from the Urengoy gas field in Siberia to the town of Uzgorod on the Czech-Soviet border; to be capable of delivering 2.8 billion feet-per-day of natural gas to Western Europe; and to cost twenty-two billion dollars.[1] The origins of the pipeline can be traced to 1968, when Soviet gas exports had commenced to five Western European recipients—Finland, Austria, France, West Germany, and Italy. In the mid–1970's a project involving Iran, the Soviet Union, and West Germany began planning the pipeline, and although the Iranians dropped out in 1978, the Soviets and Germans decided to proceed. The Soviets engaged in "intensive negotiations" with governments, financial institutions, gas utilities, and steel pipe and construction equipment firms in the United Kingdom, West Germany, France, Italy, Belgium, the Netherlands, Austria, Spain, and the United States.[2] The major initial roadblocks were not the protests which occurred against the pipeline, but rather the difficulty of obtaining the sizable amount of hard cash necessary for the project from financial institutions.[3]

During summer 1981, the Soviet Union contracted with engineering firms in France, West Germany, and Italy to obtain much of the equipment needed to build the pipeline, and these West European nations provided considerable export financing. In fall 1981 American Under Secretary of State for Economic Affairs Myer Rashish and a group of government officials visited Western Europe and tried to persuade these nations not to contract for Soviet gas. Rashish presented a set of energy alternatives, including American coal and synthetic fuels, nuclear power, African and North Sea gas, and even OPEC oil (given an expected glut). But this package of alternatives "received a polite but brusque hearing in Western Europe," which found the alternatives less appealing than a Soviet gas supply.[4] So in late 1981 and early 1982 several West European nations signed long-term gas supply contracts with the Soviet Union based on the new pipeline.

While many assume that the Soviet natural gas pipeline would create heavy West European energy dependence on the Soviet Union[5]—that West Germany, Italy, and France might receive up to thirty-five percent of their gas supplies or six percent of their total primary energy consumption from the Soviet Union—this impact and the consequent vulnerability to disruption depend on fluctuating consumption levels and supply sources.[6] The Europeans have argued that their expanded energy relationship with the Soviet Union would be "neither harmful nor unequal."[7] The Netherlands has traditionally supplied the bulk of Western Europe's gas needs, but that nation's reserves are heavily depleted and its gas prices have been rising fast; the gas from the Soviet pipeline is inexpensive by comparison and might boost the "chronically depressed" steel and engineering industries in Western Europe.[8] However, the United States government has contended that European participation in the Soviet gas pipeline project was economically unwise because (1) the resulting gas imports cross the threshold of "prudent dependence" on the Soviet Union; (2) the financing offered subsidizes

Soviet economic development; and (3) the Soviet hard currency earnings alleviate Soviet resource constraints on importing Western goods and high technology.[9]

On December 30, 1981, in response to Soviet support for martial law in Poland and the imprisonment of Solidarity officials (described in chapter three), the United States suspended licensing of American oil and gas equipment and technology for export to the Soviet Union. American companies could not help with construction of the pipeline, and the Reagan Administration suspended the licenses of Caterpillar Tractor and General Electric needed for the export of pipeline equipment. When an economic summit with European leaders at Versailles on June 6, 1982 failed to restrain Western Europe from granting further credit subsidies to the Soviets, President Reagan escalated the American embargo on June 18th to include American corporations' subsidiaries and license holders in France, Germany, Italy, and the United Kingdom. The United States claimed that these sanctions would delay the full use of the pipeline by as much as two years—to 1988—[10] but the reality may have been closer to a few months.[11] In angry response to this "extraterritorial" imposition of sanctions, in July and August France, Italy, and the United Kingdom ordered pipeline suppliers under their jurisdiction to defy the American ban. In September, the Reagan Administration imposed an export embargo on these companies. Finally, after weeks of negotiation to find a face-saving alternative for both Western Europe and the United States, on November 13th Reagan lifted all of the sanctions against the pipeline in exchange for a European commitment to "review" related issues.[12]

United States' Goals and Strategies

The American objectives in the Soviet gas pipeline controversy seemed to evolve over time. Initially, the United States stressed the goal of preventing European energy dependence on the Soviet Union; then emphasized the goal of upholding political morality, using the pipeline sanctions to condemn repression in Poland; and finally focused on the goal of eliminating the "boon to the Soviet war machine" provided by Western technology, subsidized credit, and hard-currency infusions.[13] West European states that refused to support the American pipeline position stood accused of "knowingly putting themselves under Soviet economic leverage and political influence, betraying the Polish people, and aiding the Soviet military build-up."[14]

The American strategies for pursuing these goals were (1) the use of economic sanctions against the Soviets through American multinational corporations and their subsidiaries and licensees and (2) the application of intense verbal lobbying to persuade the West Europeans to change their position on the pipeline. This United States lobbying included not only presenting counter-arguments, contradictory information, and alternative energy possibilities, but also attempting to alter the global energy picture so as to influence the Europeans' decision on the pipeline: German sources reported[15] that the Americans were "planning to exploit their own natural gas deposits in order to bring down the world market price and force the Europeans to look for alternative suppliers."

United States' Irrationality

After launching the economic sanctions in December 1981, the United States appeared to exhibit stick-in-the-mud irrationality for the duration of the controversy, until the sanctions were lifted in November 1982. Despite the overwhelming and increasing opposition from West European allies—combined with the growing evidence of (1) the sanctions' ineffectiveness in impeding the Soviet pipeline, (2) the losses incurred by American corporations, and (3) "the appalling prospect of interminable legal battles" in attempts to penalize those defying the sanctions—[16] the United States persisted in its attempt to apply and even extend the sanctions for almost a year after their initiation. This underreactive, insensitive continuation and embellishment of inappropriate policy brings to mind the American policy quagmire in the Vietnam war and epitomizes stick-in-the-mud characteristics.

United States policy concerning the Soviet gas pipeline involves three of the four dimensions of irrationality—inconsistency of statements and/or actions, non-comprehensive search-and-evaluation, and incompatibility of decisions with goals, consensus, or outcomes. There were two stages of inconsistency of statements and/or actions.

In the summer and fall of 1981, prior to the imposition of economic sanctions, the United States seemed to be "professing one thing and doing another," verbally pressuring the West Europeans not to cooperate with construction of the Soviet pipeline while doing little itself to back up its words:

> Administrative lobbying against the pipeline has been so loud that one hardly hears that American companies will be instrumental in building the pipeline and that the Administration is doing little to prevent it. Last summer, when the U.S. was arguing publicly against the project, the Commerce Department quietly issued export licenses to Caterpillar Tractor Company for pipe-laying equipment that the Russians need to build the line. (The license specified that the pipelayers were not to be used on the gas pipeline, a cosmetic provision that a Commerce official conceded was unenforceable.) The Soviets have already bought turbine engines made under license from General Electric Company. And the *New York Times* reports that 'under pressure from business, the Commerce Department is making progress simplifying its licensing procedures on exports to the Soviet Union.'[17]

In a later stage of controversy, after the imposition of economic sanctions, the United States displayed inconsistency in restricting pipeline technology and simultaneously providing grain to the Soviet Union. Joffe best describes the contradiction here:

> The Europeans were quick to rub in the inconsistency.... The Allies took endless pleasure in poking holes in the Administration's defense of its grain sales to the Soviet Union. How could trade be cynical business-as-usual when countenanced by France, Germany, or Italy, while its American counterpart was touted as a strategic advance for the West? Why was deference to the ailing steel industry in Europe more sinful than President Reagan's appeasement of Midwestern farmers beset by overproduction and falling prices—and in an election year to boot?
> It was indeed ironic that, on October 15, the U.S. Customs Service seized $3 million worth of pipeline equipment bound

for the Soviet Union while, on the same day, the President announced his readiness to sell 23 million tons of grain to the Soviet Union. That quantity represented a threefold increase over existing contract obligations.[18]

As is readily apparent, both of these inconsistencies were particularly vexing to West European allies.

Non-comprehensive search-and-evaluation also occurred at differing stages of the pipeline controversy. One flaw in the decision-making process leading to the initial sanctions in December 1981 was the gross American miscalculation, reflecting wishful thinking, of European reaction to this move: "Clearly Reagan either misjudged or simply decided to ignore the potential strength of the opposition to his stance and the consequences of disregarding these views."[19] A report released by the Office of Technology Assessment in November 1981 had indicated that American pipeline sanctions might be ineffective without Western and Japanese cooperation,[20] but this report must have been ignored. The escalation of the restrictions in June 1982 involved a further inadequacy in the policy process—the United States not only did not consult with its European allies at the Versailles summit immediately beforehand about these new sanctions, but also did not even present the issues at the summit in such a way that the expanded restrictions seemed reasonable consequences of the summit's failure.[21] Indeed, the June sanctions may not have been the product of careful, considered analysis:

> Even worse, there remained a nagging suspicion that the escalation of June 18 was not wholly triggered by considerations of grand strategy. Instead, the second wave of sanctions may have been the ad hoc product of presidential pique and intra-bureaucratic powerplays. In the aftermath of the Versailles Summit, there was an angry president who felt betrayed by his allies. And there were some key players in the Administration who seized on the President's ire to turn it into a hatchet against a detested Secretary of State.[22]

Moreover, throughout the pipeline controversy the Reagan Administration seemed somewhat out of touch with prevailing realities, displaying a "surprising lack of pragmatism"—Reagan may have actually believed that the Soviet Union was "on the point of economic collapse and that withholding Western technology and equipment from the pipeline project could hasten this collapse or at least force Moscow to take a more moderate stand on Poland and other international issues."[23]

Finally, American policy on the pipeline issue demonstrated incompatibility of decisions with goals, consensus, and preferred outcomes. The American business community, as well as much of the foreign policy-making community, was uniformly opposed to the pipeline sanctions, unhappy as usual with the politicization of profitable economic transactions. The decision to impose the sanctions did not seem logically to have much chance of contributing to the objective of the policy: "the means employed by the Reagan Administration clearly subverted the end."[24] There appear to have been strategies other than the sanctions which at the time would have been more prudent choices, in terms of foreseeable consequences, as ways of fostering positive outcomes or avoiding negative ones.

Outcome of Irrationality Use

The American policies toward the Soviet natural gas pipeline failed to achieve their objectives, as the decision in November 1982 perhaps most graphically illustrates. The pipeline sanctions caused a major rift between the United States and Western Europe, which "unified the West Europeans and strengthened their determination to resist the content and method of implementation of a U.S. policy they find utterly unreasonable"; simultaneously, the sanctions handed the Soviets "a political success they could not have dreamed of achieving by their own efforts."[25] Furthermore, the sanctions have created billions of dollars worth of losses from existing and potential contracts of American multinational corporations and their subsidiaries. The American pipeline policy was, in sum, "the flop of the year" and "a blunder of almost historic proportions."[26] The unwillingness to modify or re-evaluate when the handwriting was on the wall about the policy's ineptitude contributed to the policy disaster which ensued.

THE AMERICAN HARASSMENT OF NICARAGUA

The current American involvement in Nicaragua has its origins at the turn of the century. After a legacy of dictatorships and civil war in the nineteenth century, the United States under President Taft helped sponsor an insurgency movement in Nicaragua in 1909. A series of puppet rulers governed the nation until 1933, accompanied by the almost uninterrupted occupation of the country by American marines. In the early 1930's the United States faced a costly guerrilla campaign in Nicaragua headed by General Augusto Cesar Sandino and so withdrew, and the government became controlled by General Anastasio Somoza in 1933. Somoza's rule continued until his assassination in 1956, but the Somoza family retained control afterwards. On July 19, 1979 a revolution by the Sandinista National Liberation Front (FSLN) succeeded in overthrowing the Somoza government. The Sandinistas had been fighting the repressive Somoza regime for almost twenty years, but it was only in 1978—after the assassination of Pedro Joaquin Chamorro-Cardenal—that the urban population began to provide "active support" for the anti-Somoza struggle.[27] The core of the Sandinistas was Marxist, but a "pluralistic spirit" initially prevailed, involving non-Marxists in an alliance of political parties, labor unions, businessmen, students, and professionals.[28]

The United States under Jimmy Carter had been opposed to Somoza on human rights grounds and had been supporting moderate opposition groups, and so when the Sandinistas took over, Carter continued American aid in the hope of influencing the new regime. In March 1980, there was an upsurge of turmoil in El Salvador, and the Sandinistas backed the leftist forces there, so the United States cut off aid to Nicaragua. The Reagan Administration pressed even more vigorously for the Sandinistas to end their support of the Salvadorean leftists, but made no progress. In December 1981, it is widely believed that Reagan secretly authorized a twenty-million-dollar CIA plan to create a paramilitary force based in Honduras designed to cut off Nicaraguan supplies to the Salvadorean leftists.

On March 15, 1982, the friction between the United States and Nicaragua reached a peak, as the Sandinistas declared a "state of siege" because of American-backed raids from Honduras perceived as designed to overthrow the Sandinista government. In August 1982 American planes flew Honduran troops to the Nicaraguan border to protect anti-Sandinista forces, and the United States increased substantially its aid to Honduras in 1983. By 1984 there were 8,000 men in the Nicaraguan Democratic Force (FDN), commonly called "contras" for counter-revolutionaries, openly financed, armed, and directed by the United States and operating from behind the protective shield of the Honduras border.[29] In these same years the United States staged major military exercises around Honduras, including naval maneuvers on both sides of the isthmus, to communicate resolve about opposition to leftists in Central America. The United States also imposed economic sanctions on Nicaragua, culminating in a total trade embargo, and made it difficult for Nicaragua to obtain loans from international financial institutions, thus creating a critical shortage of hard currency.[30] Politically, President Reagan since taking office has "attempted to foster regional political alliances isolating Nicaragua."[31] Meanwhile Cuba was sending Nicaragua many military advisors, along with doctors and technicians, and the Sandinistas were beginning to display open admiration for the Castro regime. The Soviet Union also provided significant military aid. In April 1984, the "secret war" again reached a climax point following revelations that the CIA had directed the mining of Nicaraguan harbors, damaging ships of several nations including a Soviet tanker.

At least some analysts believe that the threat to Nicaragua from internal problems is as great as that from outside agitation by the United States. Arturo Cruz, former Nicaraguan ambassador to the United States (and now a supporter of the contras), summarizes his view of the internal conditions:

The Sandinista leaders as guerrillas were authentic classics—daring, shrewd, flawless. . . . They have not proved successful statesmen and are overwhelmed by the responsibilities of government, which they render more complex by their own dogmatism. After 45 months of Sandinista rule, the nation is in a calamitous state. The people are divided by hatred and resentment, the economy is in a shambles, and a war rages, threatening to reach the level of intensity that existed when Somoza was put at bay.[32]

Even before Reagan's covert operations had a serious impact on the Nicaraguan economy, "the country was on the verge of bankruptcy by early 1982," due to the "socioeconomic failure" produced by the Sandinistas' "good intentions, incompetence, and narrow sectarianism."[33] In May 1982 the heaviest rain in decades hit western Nicaragua, causing massive flooding and three hundred and fifty million dollars worth of damage and "a much darker panorama" for Nicaragua's economic (and political) future.[34]

United States' Goals and Strategies

American goals in Nicaragua have undergone significant change over time. For most of the pre-Sandinista period, American objectives were dominated by economic interests in Nicaragua's agricultural and mineral resources, along with concerns about building a canal through Lake Nicaragua; but then "Washington's earlier concern for the defense of private economic interests has been replaced by a preoccupation with Nicaragua as a pawn on the East-West chessboard."[35] Within the framework of a Cold War dispute, the United States has gradually "moved away from the narrow question of Sandinista interference in its neighbors' affairs and began insisting on major changes in the basic nature of the Sandinista regime itself."[36] Although the United States often states its goal as opposition to Sandinista aid to the El Salvadorean leftist guerrilla movement, the Reagan Administration may, at least in some analysts' eyes, be "seeking nothing less than the overthrow of the Sandinist government."[37] These objectives seem to be founded on the American government's belief that Nicaragua is a "platform of war and terror in the region,"[38] seeing "the Sandinistas as carriers of a revolutionary virus that came from the Soviet Union by way of Cuba, and with which they will surely attempt to infect the rest of Central America."[39] While parts of the American government certainly differ from the President's extreme position on the goals in Nicaragua, Reagan's interpretation has by-and-large been the most influential in terms of policies actually undertaken.

The strategies involved in the pursuit of these goals encompass the combination of military, political, and economic instruments outlined earlier. The paramilitary activities are the most controversial, and serious questions have emerged about the limits of American involvement. President Reagan has stated that "there is no thought of sending American combat troops to Central America," but by the end of 1983 this was "an increasingly tenuous assumption" due to the ineffectiveness of the anti-Sandinista rebels.[40] Indeed, the Nicaraguans "are convinced that the Reagan Administration would like nothing more than to promote a full-scale war between themselves and Honduras, one that Nicaragua would appear to have started, as a pretext for direct military action."[41] Politically, the United States' pressure on governments to support American policies has placed "additional weight" on already "sorely-strained" alliances.[42] Political initiatives by other nations—whether it be the twenty-one-point framework for peace endorsed in September 1983 by the Contadora group of Mexico, Venezuela, Colombia, and Panama, or the moderate proposals of the Sandinistas themselves—have been largely rejected or ignored by the United States.[43] Economic measures appear to be the United States' "least confrontational" weapon, but threats continue of more severe sanctions.[44] A principal underlying theme in all of these aspects of current American strategy in Nicaragua involves the notion of symmetry:

In its most basic form, symmetry was aptly summed up by a senior U.S. diplomat in Central America as 'trading one little war for another little war.' If Nicaraguan-backed guerrillas in El Salvador attacked the bases of the Salvadoran economy, then the United States would support guerrillas in Nicaragua attacking the bases of the Nicaraguan economy. An eye for an eye, an oil storage depot for an oil storage depot, as it were. If the Salvadoran guerrillas demanded that negotiations lead to their participation as equal partners in the Salvadoran government, then the Nicaraguan guerrillas, or 'counterrevolutionaries' or 'contras', as they were called, made the same demand on the Sandinistas.[45]

United States' Irrationality

Even though controversy and ambiguity are pervasive in this confrontation, it appears that the United States under the Reagan Administration has displayed stick-in-the-mud irrationality in its harassment of Nicaragua. Despite new initiatives from the Sandinistas and Contadoras, unanticipated effects of American moves, and changing circumstances in the region, the United States has persisted in a fixed "big stick" policy. Gleijeses[46] calls this under-reactive policy "sterile," and claims that it is the preferred policy because Reagan and his advisors would rather hope for a Sandinista collapse (wishful thinking) than "accept a reality they consider humiliating." The prevailing assumption that Sandinista statements have no credibility serves to reinforce this stagnant policy, as well as to imply "that it is fruitless to seek regional peace by means of negotiations, for the Sandinistas will break any agreement they sign."[47]

All four dimensions of irrationality emerge in this case—non-dispassionate style of decision, non-comprehensive search-and-evaluation, incompatibility of decisions with goals, consensus, or outcomes, and inconsistency of statements and/or actions. With regard to the first dimension of emotionalism, Ullman[48] asserts that "it may be asking too much to expect such dispassionate reflection from Mr. Reagan and his colleagues" because "they are too committed" and are "unlikely, unassisted, to find their way out of the web their paranoia has spun." There is general agreement that "a visceral reaction warps the administration's thinking" on this issue,[49] involving deep and consistent hostility which is manifested in many ways and pursued aggressively.[50] The policy appears to some to be downright "obsessive," and may demonstrate "a frame of mind that future historians are likely to discuss more in terms of pathology than in those of logic."[51]

The non-comprehensive search-and-evaluation by American policy makers is largely evident in their profound misunderstanding—often based on inadequate information—of the situation in Nicaragua. Calling Nicaragua "totalitarian"[52] or "Marxist Nicaragua"[53] is an example of these oversimplified misconceptions. The United States exaggerates the extent to which Nicaragua can be manipulated by outside forces,[54] as well as the real level of political and military threat posed by Nicaragua,[55] and ignores "as irrelevant ancient history the fact that many Nicaraguans feel that the Sandinistas liberated themselves as much from the interventionist hand of the United States as from a harsh dictatorship that exploited the entire country as its private plantation."[56] The decision-making problem here is rooted in "the all-too-familiar predilection of junior officers to send up the line what they know their superiors want to hear"—"one thing their seniors have not wanted to hear about is the existence of possibilities of diplomatic solutions."[57]

Several of the American decisions on Nicaragua have appeared to be incompatible with strong Congressional feeling, if not consensus, against actions taken. Many members of both Houses of Congress—a majority of Democrats and a considerable minority of Republicans—"feel the Administration's policies are profoundly misguided."[58] But Congress has so far been unable to mobilize effectively this opposition: "If Congress has evinced clear misgivings about Reagan's policy toward Nicaragua . . . it has also evinced a complete inability to devise, much less impose, an alternative policy, seeking instead refuge in disgruntled passivity."[59] This disgruntlement, when combined with that from academics and some church groups in the United States, represents considerable sentiment in this country contending against the Administration viewpoint.

Finally, there has been some inconsistency of statements and actions in the Nicaraguan affair. Ullman points out one example, which hints at the possibility of intentional transmission of disinformation:

The Administration has assured Congress that the counter-revolutionary"freedom fighters' strike at military targets. Reality is different. On a tour of rural development projects in August I saw farm buildings devastated by mortar fire or by the torch. And I heard many accounts of peasant families being kidnapped and taken across the border, often never to return, and of assassinated teachers, health workers, and agricultural technicians.[60]

Outcome of Irrationality Use

The outcome of American policy in Nicaragua has up to this point been largely failure. While Nicaragua has been forced to focus on internal problems, the situation in El Salvador seems to be improving, and American actions "have made life in Sandinist Nicaragua more grim than it otherwise might be," these trends "will not be sufficient to undermine the regime" because of "the loyalty and the support" of the peasants and the salaried rural and urban workers.[61] The Sandinistas have been "consolidating their grip on Nicaragua," and the United States has not been able "to generate any very decisive results" in the confrontation.[62] Given the resentment of American moves, at least one analyst[63] concludes that "the policies now being pursued by the Administration will lead to exactly the outcome that will be most harmful to the long-term interests of the United States." All four dimensions of American stick-in-the-mud irrationality, but particularly the non-dispassionate style of decision and the non-comprehensive search-and-evaluation, seem to have prevented the success of American military, economic, and political actions in Nicaragua.

THE SOMALI TERRITORIAL DISPUTE

Long before Somalia became independent in 1960, the country served as a staging area for the invasion and conquest of Ethiopia during the Italo-Ethiopian conflict of 1935–36. More recently, the overthrow of Ethiopia's government of Emperor Haile Selassie in 1974 triggered massive turmoil in the region. Somalia viewed the confusion following the revolution as a golden opportunity to attempt to liberate the neighboring Somali-inhabited portion of Ethiopia—the Ogaden desert region—so as "to realize in part the commitment to Pan-Somali unification embedded in the Constitution at independence."[64] Meanwhile, other nationalist groups within Ethiopia, such as the Tigre Liberation Front and the Oromo Liberation Front, also began to press their claims against the new "Marxist" government there.

As a result of these tensions, as well as of a dispute over recently independent Djibouti, the Ogaden War broke out in July 1977 between Ethiopia and Somalia. The Ethiopians, receiving several billion dollars worth of arms from the Soviet Union[65] and aided by Cuban forces, defeated the Somalis in March 1978. Despite the decisive outcome of the war, fighting has "continued almost incessantly" since that time between the two nations.[66]

The latest wave of fighting commenced in July 1982. President Siad Barre of Somalia, despite his claim that his country was "homogeneous in every respect,"[67] had been having some internal tribal problems: two critical northern tribes—the Issak and the Majeerteen—were accusing Barre of favoring his own tribe (the Marehan) in the south, even though the north is much richer and pays most of the taxes.[68] These accusations had resulted in violent rioting in early 1982. Furthermore, these dissident tribes supported Ethiopia-based guerrilla groups opposed to the Somali government—the Issak supported the Somali National Movement (SNM), and the Majeerteen supported the Somali Democratic Salvation Front (SDSF). In July the SDSF invaded Somalia with 30,000 men, occupied two Somali border towns, and has not as yet been dislodged; then in January 1983 the SNM raided a Somali jail in the northwest and allegedly released over seven hundred prisoners.[69] There is considerable disagreement over who exactly is now fighting: "The Ethiopians deny any involvement, claiming that the offensive was launched by Somali dissidents"; while the Somalis say that the invading force consisted of Ethiopian regulars, Cubans running the tanks and armored cars, South Yemeni and East German pilots flying the planes, Russian advisors coordinating the whole operation, and Libyans financing it.[70] The generally accepted motivation for this attack was that the Somali dissident groups within Ethiopia had miscalculated and had "convinced its military that Somali feeling against President Siad Barre had reached the point where an invading force would be received as liberators."[71] Meanwhile, Somalia has actively supported its own guerrilla group—the Western Somali Liberation Front (WSLF)—which is fighting continuously with the Ethiopians over control of the Ogaden.

The economic and humanitarian impact of the conflict has been staggering. The Ogaden War has created a half million to a million refugees for Somalia, representing an enormous burden for a country traditionally ranked one of the twenty-five poorest in the world.[72] In 1980, the Somalis contended that one-fourth of their population consisted of refugees from the Ogaden.[73] The annual bill for food alone for the refugees is eighty-seven million dollars, and international humanitarian aid is woefully inadequate due to the continuing, "semipermanent" nature of the problem.[74]

This conflict in the Horn of Africa has attracted considerable attention from nations outside of the region. As Arnold[75] aptly asserts, "The basic Western concern with the refugees may be humanitarian, but the size of the problem and the inputs required make this Western involvement a highly political one." There has been a rapid growth in outside assistance to Somalia in the last few years: major new donors include the United States, West Germany, Italy, the European Economic Community, China, Saudi Arabia, and other Gulf states, the total annual flow of aid reaching four hundred million dollars, or forty percent of the Somali gross national product.[76] However, this situation "ignores the country's lack of infrastructure and absorptive capacity for aid on such a scale," and "in the long run, the results could be disastrous."[77]

The United States faces a particular dilemma with respect to the Somali-Ethiopia conflict—"how to support an anti-Soviet government whose expulsion of the Russians in 1977 was followed by an appeal to Washington for help, without alienating other regional allies or closing the door to some future cooperation with Ethiopia, many of whose military rulers were trained in the United States prior to the Revolution."[78] The United States "would undoubtedly like to regain the position it once held in Ethiopia, whose large population and strategic location near the Red Sea and Sudan is seen as far more important than Somalia's assets, despite the latter's huge coastline on the Red Sea and Indian Ocean."[79] Former American ambassador to the United Nations Andrew Young describes American resistance to Somali pressure to intervene in the conflict:

> Certainly, the Horn is of strategic importance to the United States with regard to commercial and military routes, but even today it is difficult to discern any strategic interest in spending millions of dollars to compete with the Soviets in a battle for a thousand miles of sand. That is, U.S. interest in Somali bases would not justify involvement in the battle for the Ogaden desert region held by Ethiopia and coveted by Somalia.[80]

Nonetheless, the United States is rehabilitating the Somali port facilities at Berbera, has about forty military personnel in the country, and has substantially increased its aid to Somalia over the past few years—covering such areas as agriculture, health, water, commodity support for timber, as well as refugee assistance—totaling one hundred and twenty million dollars worth of ongoing projects.[81] Moreover, in August 1983 American marines joined the Somali army for Operation East Wind, a war game in Somalia designed to help the country in its self-defense.

Somalia's Goals and Strategies

Somali policy goals in the ongoing conflict appear to be somewhat "vague": "Somalia has adopted a policy—that the refugees from the Ogaden are autonomous people and Somalia must help them maintain their semi-independent status in relation to Addis Ababa— that lies midway between war to regain the territory and renunciation of its claims."[82] An accompanying objective is "to maximize U.S. support in the area so as to strengthen the Somali position in relation to Ethiopia."[83] Secondary Somali goals are seeking Western economic aid and achieving voluntary repatriation and resettlement of refugees in Somalia.[84] The goal of the WSLF is much more clearly reasserting Somali control in the Ogaden,[85] but in recent years the WSLF and the Somali government have been increasingly divergent in their objectives.[86]

In order to attract Western support, Somali strategy is to focus world attention on, and probably exaggerate, the threat from Ethiopia. This approach plays "naturally upon Washington's sensitivity to Soviet, Cuban, or Libyan activities."[87] In order to achieve their objectives in the Ogaden region, Somali military tactics are to continue to support the WSLF guerrillas and to continue military readiness against further Ethiopian, SDSF, or SNM intrusions.

Somalia's Irrationality

Somalia's policy toward Ethiopia with respect to the Ogaden territorial dispute reflects consistent stick-in-the-mud irrationality.

Despite the decisive loss in the 1977–78 war, the absence of strong international support, and severe internal economic hardships, Somalia continues refusing to make significant changes in its policies or to renounce or modify its pursuit of territorial claims. President Barre "urgently needs a stable peace with Ethiopia,"[88] but this need has had no major impact on policy. Mayall best sums up Somalia's underreactive intransigence:

> Both the Ethiopian and Somalian governments periodically express an interest in political solution, but it is always on their own terms. Since no one can afford to make a major concession, there is no obvious end to the violence in sight.
> How is this depressing immobility to be explained? The short answer is that domestic, regional, and external pressures combine to keep the Horn at once in a state of turmoil, with governments under constant pressure at home and abroad, and, in the final analysis, to support the status quo.[89]

Thus Ethiopia and Somalia seem to be locked into long-term strife with no escape.

Of the four dimensions of irrationality, Somalia most blatantly exhibits inconsistency of statements and actions. The Somali government displays hypocrisy about its basic aims in the dispute: "Although the Somali government often insists that it has no territorial claims—instead the new 1979 Constitution commits the state to support 'the liberation of Somali territory under colonial oppression'—African governments are openly skeptical of Somalia's colonial thesis."[90] A related inconsistency reflects "a certain irony in the situation" where "President Barre is complaining of aggression across a border he refuses to accept exists."[91] Furthermore, Somalia officially denies many of the sporadic confrontations which occur between Somali and Ethiopian forces.[92] Finally, Somalia exaggerates its actual successes in the ongoing conflict:

> New arrivals at the Mogadishu airport are greeted by a brightly coloured portrait of a Somali soldier in full battledress which states "Somalia has succeeded in repelling the foreign invader." Well, almost.[93]

So many half-truths have circulated about the origins and status of the ongoing conflict that it is indeed difficult to separate myth from reality.

Outcome of Irrationality Use

The Somali stick-in-the-mud policy in the territorial dispute with Ethiopia has so far failed. The outcome of the conflict itself has been a stalemate in the fighting, with no resolution forthcoming.[94] Barre is "unable to renew the war in the Ogaden in order to achieve 'Greater Somalia', nor can the government afford to renounce its claims."[95] While the Ethiopian invasion has brought "increased public support for the president," the conflict has clearly not managed "to calm northern dissatisfaction."[96] The entire region has suffered "disintegration of the social, political and indeed ecological systems," and Somalia has experienced "diplomatic isolation" in Africa, with little support from the Organization of African Unity and prospects for future support bleak.[97] Somalia has recently received more American arms support, but not nearly as much as Barre would like; the American response to Barre's appeals for arms "can only be described as slow and minimal."[98] Finally, there are few signs that repatriation of refugees is occurring or that their needs have been effectively addressed.[99] Somalia has "had to turn to the International Monetary Fund and has agreed to two devaluations," and is also in the midst of a debt crisis.[100] The inability of Somalia to adapt its policies to changing external circumstances, along with its inconsistent policy pronouncements lacking credibility, certainly has helped to precipitate failure in this confrontation.

SYNTHESIS

In the three cases described in this chapter, the initiating nation employed a basically coercive, compellent approach to achieve a change in the status quo, after having previously been unable to prevent the existing undesirable status quo from occurring. The United States, having failed to convince the Europeans to oppose the Soviet natural gas pipeline, tried to force disruption of the pipeline construction through economic sanctions; and having failed to keep the Sandinistas out of power in Nicaragua, tried to undermine the regime through a variety of military, economic, and political sanctions. Somalia, having failed to prevent Ethiopian consolidation of control of the Ogaden in the 1977–78 war, tried to force some level of semi-autonomy for the region through support of guerrillas. Stick-in-the-mud irrationality appears to be unsuccessful when used to pursue non-status-quo ends in situations where the initiating state has previously been unsuccessful in forestalling the current situation in the target state. This ineffectiveness seems to be the consequence even when the initiating nation is much more powerful than the target. The roots of this failure appear to lie in (1) the coalescence of opposition to the initiating state at the time it tries to prevent the undesirable situation from occurring in the first place; and (2) the subsequent low reputation for resolve and credibility of threat of the initiating state when it uses stick-in-the-mud coercion to attempt to alter these circumstances after they have already occurred.

A closely related impediment to the effectiveness of stick-in-the-mud irrationality in these cases is that the goals of the initiating nation are either vague or waffling or undergo significant change in the course of the confrontation, while the strategies remain stagnant. The United States in both the pipeline and Nicaragua cases had its goals become increasingly broad, hardline, and linked to the Cold War, while Somalia has been more of the unclear waffler in its dispute with Ethiopia. The lack of unambiguous and stable objectives makes it difficult for a process like stick-in-the-mud irrationality, which depends on persistence in wearing down of the opponent, to be effective in achieving desired ends.

Given these severe drawbacks, a coercive use of stick-in-the-mud irrationality to change the status quo seems most successful when the initiating country can and does employ the full range of strategies—military, political, and economic—as the United States has done in Nicaragua; rather than when the initiating country only employs a narrower range of strategies, as the United States did in the pipeline confrontation (mostly economic and some political) or Somalia has done in the Ethiopia conflict (mostly military and some political). The greater the variety of strategies used to comprise the stick-in-the-mud approach in these cases, the more likely it seems that one of the strategies will not link up in the target's eyes to the initiator's past failure, and thus the more likely the disconnected strategy seems to communicate credibility and resolve. However, even with the full range of strategies, stick-in-the-mud irrationality that involves direct coercion to reverse a previously (and vainly) opposed status quo appears to be rarely effective.

5.

"Daredevil" Irrationality—
Successes

The third set of case studies exhibit daredevil irrationality and have relatively successful outcomes. The confrontations studied are the Iranian seizure of American hostages, the Soviet involvement in the Korean Airlines incident, and the American invasion of Grenada. Each case involves an unexpected violent move within or near one's own territory designed to assert national resolve in the face of a perceived international challenge.

THE IRANIAN SEIZURE OF AMERICAN HOSTAGES

The seizure of the American embassy personnel in Tehran has roots tracing back to the beginning of the Shah's rule in Iran. In 1921, Colonel Reza Pahlavi attained power in Iran through a military coup and initiated a program combining modernization and repression of opposition. In 1951 the National Front, a nationalistic Islamic movement, brought Mohammad Mossadeq into power. In August 1953, pro-Shah Iranian generals and the CIA launched a successful military coup against Mossadeq, and the Shah returned to power.

In 1963 Shi'ite Muslim leader Ayatollah Ruhollah Khomeini was an outspoken critic of the Pahlavi regime and "had already achieved such importance as an activist religious leader that the government sent security forces into his theological college in Qum on March 22, 1963."[1] Finally, in November 1964, Khomeini was exiled from

Iran for his interference in political matters, especially his attacks on Iranian ties to the West and on extending diplomatic immunity to increasing numbers of American advisers in Iran.

In 1975, the Iranian economy began to experience a downturn, and the gap grew between the wealthy urban elite and the rural poor. Throughout most of 1978 protests and rioting occurred in Iran, and a broad alliance of intellectuals, merchants, Marxists, students, and Muslim clergy organized against the Shah. On September 7, 1978, the Shah imposed martial law in Tehran and eleven other cities. In November, the Shah created a military government and Khomeini—in exile in Paris—called on the army to revolt. On December 30th the Shah directed an opposition leader, Shahpur Bakhtiar, to form a civilian government. In January 1979 the Shah left Iran for a "vacation," while Khomeini urged resistance to the Bakhtiar government. On February lst Khomeini returned to Iran, appointed Mehdi Bazargan to succeed Bakhtiar, and later that month attacked and overcame the Shah's army. In March, a popular referendum showed overwhelming support for the Khomeini government.

On October 19, 1979 the United States agreed to the Shah's admission to that country and informed the Iranian government that the stay was temporary and for medical reasons. On November lst, Khomeini denounced the Shah's admission to the United States and directed Iranian students to expand efforts to force the Americans to return the Shah to Iran. Finally, on November 4th, militant Muslim students stormed the American embassy in Tehran and seized ninety hostages, of whom sixty-three were American, and threatened not to release them until the Shah was returned for trial.

Most of the hostages were held for four hundred and forty-four days, until their release on January 20, 1981. The United States quickly responded in November 1979 by halting imports of Iranian oil and freezing Iranian assets in American banks. The United Nations intervened in the situation with no success. President Carter "evoked almost universal international support for his refusal to allow Khomeini to coerce this country by holding Americans for ransom," and even the Soviet Union, which was concerned about the vulnerability of its own embassies, "officially" supported the United States.[2] On December 15th the Shah left the United States for Panama, and on March 23, 1980 he left Panama for Egypt in a dispute over medical care. On April 7th the United States severed diplomatic relations with Iran and embargoed exports to Iran, and on April 24th attempted an abortive helicopter rescue of the American hostages. On July 27th the Shah died in Egypt, and on September 12th Khomeini softened the terms of the hostage release by focusing mainly on an economic settlement. On September 22nd the Iran-Iraq War broke out (discussed in chapter six) and delayed hostage talks. On November 3rd Iran chose Algeria as an intermediary in the negotiations, and after much bargaining there was finally agreement on the terms of release on January 18, 1981. The negotiation was difficult throughout because "the multiplicity of power centers in Tehran made serious dialogue impossible,"[3] particularly with the hostages being held by "a group of student radicals not under the clear control of any civilian authority."[4] The wide differences in values and reasoning styles also promoted intractability.

Iran's Goals and Strategies

The specific goals of the Khomeini regime underwent transition in the midst of the hostage crisis. Initially, in November 1979, the objectives were "the return of the Shah for trial and a formal American apology for American 'crimes' in Iran"; but in September 1980 these ends changed to include (1) the return of the Shah's American wealth, (2) an American pledge of noninterference in Iran, (3) the release of Iranian assets, and (4) the termination of American claims against Iran.[5] Two broad underlying goals provided the framework for these immediate objectives: Khomeini's "desire to free Iran from 'the hands of the foreigners' and his desire to re-establish the preeminence of Shi'ite Islamic law in his homeland."[6] Despite his expressed objective of seeing a strong and prosperous Iran, Khomeini viewed "the validation of his mission more in terms of moral than in terms of material advancement."[7]

The strategies Khomeini used to pursue these goals were support for (and protection of) the students holding the Americans hostage, and fanning the flames of anti-Western—particularly anti-American—feelings in Iran. Rouleau explains how the hostage seizure was a well-timed tactic for Khomeini's purposes:

Indeed, it was clear from the outset that Imam Khomeini was going to utilize the widespread anti-American sentiment to mobilize the population under his banner. Popular discontent—due mainly to economic problems and the duality of power—had reached alarming proportions by October 1979. The government (along with the secular nationalists and most of the leftist parties) was preparing to resist the adoption of the draft Islamic constitution then being drawn up. The occupation of the American Embassy thus came at the perfect time, pushing divisive factors to the background and uniting the people against the Shah's protectors. The same mechanism applied after the rescue mission of April 25: the U.S. attempt provided Khomeini with tangible evidence that the principal danger threatening the Iranian people was foreign intervention.[8]

Moreover, the hostage crisis served as a means of readily identifying enemies against the state and quieting opposition— "all those who supported the Islamic students were in the good camp, on the side of anti-imperialism and the revolution, all others could safely be labeled pro-Western counterrevolutionaries."[9] Khomeini thus provided a textbook example of manipulating the internal and external enemy image in order to unify the people and legitimize the regime.

Iran's Irrationality

The Iranian seizure of American embassy personnel was a classic case of daredevil irrationality. It involved an over-reactive and rash response, which stunned the world, to the Shah's entry into the United States. In President Carter's words, it was "an act of terrorism totally outside the bounds of international law and diplomatic tradition."[10] Even most of the Arab world felt that it was "sheer sacrilege" for Khomeini to claim he was acting in the name of Islam when he was "violating every principle of civilized conduct between nations."[11]

The primary dimensions of irrationality displayed by the Iranians during the hostage crisis were non-dispassionate style and non-comprehensive search-and-evaluation in their decision making. The level of emotionalism involved was virtually unmatched in any other modern interstate confrontation. A portion of the venom appears to have been understandably rooted in the background conditions of the hostage affair:[12] the legacy of centuries of "occupation and humiliation by foreigners" had made "xenophobia something of a national trait" in Iran; the Shi'ite Muslims were far more fundamentalist, dogmatic, and militant than Islam's dominant sect, and placed value on martyrdom and revenge; and Khomeini's own attitude was at least partially explained by the Shah's forcing him into exile and allegedly being responsible for the death of Khomeini's father and one of his sons. But the emotional style of Khomeini and his followers went well beyond what might be expected from these origins. Khomeini's black-and-white thinking is highlighted in two representative quotations:

> All Western governments are just thieves. We should simply cut all ties to them. Nothing but evil comes from them.[13]

> All the problems of the East stem from these foreigners from the West, and from America at the moment. All our problems come from America. All the problems of the Moslems stem from America.[14]

Khomeini's belief was that his "branch of Islam is superior to all others" and that "the Moslem faith is infallible."[15]

The Ayatollah's followers similarly avoided any effort to be dispassionate. When the students first occupied the American embassy, they asked, "How can we really tolerate seeing these instigating mercenaries in our homeland, while their country has become a haven for our enemy, the murderer of hundreds of thousands of our brothers and sisters, martyred by the criminal shah?"[16] The students later told a reporter "Our cup of hatred is filled to overflowing," and some followers wanted to declare a "jihad"—holy war—against the United States.[17] Much of Iran viewed the captors of the hostages as "revolutionary heroes who defied the 'imperialism' of 'the Great Satan', the revolutionary code for the United States."[18]

The non-comprehensive search-and-evaluation relates naturally to this emotional style of decision. First, Khomeini did not consider the full range of policy options available:[19] "Khomeini is an intransigent man who, by ideological conviction as well as by temperament, brooks no half-measures"; and he "has no desire to compromise and is impervious to threats." Second, the Iranian "administration was virtually paralyzed by the inertia—voluntary or otherwise—of civil servants, many of whom no doubt consciously sought to undermine the regime."[20]

Outcome of Irrationality Use

Although mixed reactions[21] emerged to the appropriateness of American actions during the hostage crisis and to American concessions in the final settlement, there can be no real doubt that the Khomeini regime achieved some major successes through the hostage seizure. The crisis effectively focused international attention on the Shah's repressive record in Iran, helping to legitimize the new regime. Iran received relatively quickly $2.8 billion in Iranian assets held abroad which, while considerably less than initial demands, was a sizable settlement sum. The hostage affair was instrumental in the Shah's decision to leave the United States, and only his death negated the possibility of fulfilling the objective of returning him to Iran. Although the United States never did apologize to Iran, Khomeini succeeded in "humiliating" the United States, bringing a superpower to its knees in a precedent-setting manner.[22] Thus Iran's daredevil irrationality placed the United States in "a no-win situation from any standpoint,"[23] in which the American government lacked an effective arsenal of tried-and-true policy options for coping with the surprising situation.

THE KOREAN AIRLINES INCIDENT

Several details of the Soviet downing of the Korean Airlines commercial jet are still shrouded in mystery and controversy, but there is now agreement on at least many of the central features of the incident. In the early dawn of September 1, 1983, Korean Airlines Flight 007 began the last leg—from Anchorage, Alaska—of a two-day journey from New York to Seoul, South Korea. Aboard were twenty-nine crew members and two hundred and forty passengers, including sixty-one Americans. Within ten minutes, the plane began to stray from its designated route, which is the northernmost of five flight routes on the northwestern rim of the Pacific Ocean. The new route passed over the Kamchatka peninsula and near the sensitive Soviet naval base of Petropavlovsk, home to ninety nuclear-powered submarines. Soviet radar picked up an unidentified aircraft approaching Soviet airspace, and Soviet SU–15 interceptor jets went up to find it. About two and one-half hours after initial detection, the two Soviet jets caught up with the KAL Boeing 747 aircraft and, in response to an order from the regional commander of the Biya sector in the USSR, one Soviet jet (after some warning shots) fired two heat-seeking missiles and destroyed the Korean plane around Sakhalin Island. The incident involved the worst attack in history on a civilian airliner, and there were no survivors.

The Korean plane's flight recorder was lost in the crash in the Sea of Japan, preventing the resolution of some controversial questions. One debate surrounds the reason why KAL Flight 007 was off course, as it was over two hundred miles from its scheduled route when the Russians shot it down. The United States claimed the pilot made a navigational error and did not know he was over Soviet territory; the weakness in this argument is that the pilot was one of KAL's most senior ones, with 10,500 hours in command, two years experience flying this particular route, and a reputation as one of South Korea's best pilots.[24] Also the navigational coordinates can be electronically displayed and are usually cross-checked by a second crew member.[25] The Soviets asserted that the aircraft was being used as a reconnaissance plane for a spy mission to photograph sensitive military installations and/or to probe Soviet air defenses and draw fighter planes up from the ground; a later accusation appearing in the British journal *Defense Attaché* stated that "the half-hour delay in departure from Alaska allowed the Korean airliner to coordinate its path with the U.S. space shuttle [*Challenger*] then orbiting earth, so that the shuttle could measure Soviet response to the intruding aircraft."[26] The problem with the Soviet explanation is that there was no direct or indirect evidence of espionage activity by the aircraft; the space shuttle (NASA claims) "was never close enough to receive aircraft radio transmissions from the 007 intrusive area," and such a spying attempt with a commercial jet would seem foolhardy—"what pilot could be induced to risk the lives of himself and his passengers on such a brazen mission, which was certain to be detected?"[27] Thus an accusation has even emerged that the espionage contentions "are a result of 'a massive, overt disinformation campaign' by the Soviet Union."[28]

The International Civil Aviation Organization (ICAO), a United Nations organization to which one hundred fifty-one nations (including the Soviet Union) belong, issued a detailed report[29] in December 1983 evaluating the incident. The report concluded that the plane unknowingly flew off course either because its navigator punched the wrong longitude for Anchorage—one hundred forty-nine instead of one hundred thirty-nine—into the computerized navigational system, or because the navigator erroneously set the plane on a steady magnetic compass heading of two hundred forty-six degrees. However, the KAL crew members would have to have been "inexplicably careless" not to have known that the plane had drifted into Soviet airspace.[30] The ICAO rejected the spy theory, as well as theories that the plane might have been taking a short-cut to save fuel or that it might have been hijacked.[31] After an intensive two-year investigation, journalist Seymour Hersh more recently agreed that there was no spy plot and strongly argues that navigational errors—involving "ordinary human failings" of the KAL crew members and possibly faulty electronic guidance equipment—caused the plane to fly off course.[32]

A second debate focuses on whether or not the Soviets knew that they were shooting down a civilian airliner. The United States initially thought so: President Reagan condemned the Soviet Union, declaring his "disgust that the entire free world feels at the barbarity of the Soviet government in shooting down an unarmed plane" and stating "Words cannot express our revulsion at this horrifying act of violence."[33] But later the Pentagon confirmed reports that an American RC–135 spy plane, which is a converted Boeing 707, had been in the general area of the Korean aircraft—at one point only seventy-five miles from it—and thus some United States intelligence officials found more understandable the Russian perception that the jet shot down was a reconnaissance plane.[34] Because the Soviet pilot fired the rockets from behind and below KAL Flight 007, the distinctive nose hump of the Boeing 747 aircraft might not have been visible in the darkness of the night. Military experts have concluded that the Soviet Union had reason to expect an American reconnaissance mission at that time because the Soviets were test-firing a new missile there.[35] Moreover, Hersh reveals that the American National Security Agency had intercepted a Russian message indicating that the Soviets indeed thought that the jet was an American military intelligence plane.[36] But the Soviets' argument that they confused the Boeing 747 plane with the RC–135 plane is still complicated by one analyst's contention[37] that the Russians "tracked the KAL 007 and RC135 separately and knew there were two planes."

No satisfactory explanation has surfaced about why the Korean aircraft failed to respond to Soviet communication attempts and warning shots, although some assert that "the KAL pilots were aware they were being pursued and either flashed navigation lights or waggled the aircraft's wings to signal compliance."[38] The United States was in all likelihood tracking the off-course Korean jetliner, but "KAL 007 probably wasn't warned because none of the watchers thought the Russians would react by shooting it down."[39] A more sinister explanation is that "U.S. military trackers saw it go astray, issued no warning and coldly exploited the situation to see how Soviet air-defense systems would react."[40]

Soviet Union's Goals and Strategies

The Soviet Union's goal in shooting down Korean Flight 007 was the traditional obsession of Soviet political leaders with "safety from foreign invasion."[41] Russia's history of attack from outside has seemed to many to create almost a "neurosis" in this regard. The Soviets appear especially "paranoid" about protecting against "intrusions in the airspace in strategic areas."[42] Charles Lichenstein, who as deputy American envoy at the United Nations participated in a Security Council effort to denounce the Soviet Union, asserted that the Soviet objective was "intimidation" and teaching the world the lesson, "Don't mess with us."[43]

The Soviet Union claimed that its strategy in the Korean Airlines incident was to track the errant plane, attempt to contact it, fire warning shots, force the plane down, and finally—"only after the Soviet Air Defense Forces had exhausted all cautionary warning devices at their disposal—to destroy the aircraft."[44] This strategy was not new for the Soviet Union, and indeed "was only the latest and most extreme episode in a series of attacks by Soviet gunners on military and commercial planes over the last three decades:[45] recent violent confrontations in the area include the Soviets firing on a South Korean airliner crossing Soviet territory while flying from Paris to Seoul on April 20, 1978; shooting down an American plane in the Barents Sea near Kola Peninsula on July 1, 1960; and attacking a U.S. Navy patrol plane near the Sea of Japan on June 16, 1959.

Soviet Union's Irrationality

The Soviet Union's response to the Korean airliner's intrusion into Soviet airspace appears to be a manifestation of daredevil irrationality. Despite the role of standard operating procedures in the response, the history of the Soviet Union's use of force to protect its territory, and the warnings that occurred before the shooting, destroying the aircraft was a rash and overreactive policy even in the Soviet context. Outsiders generally believed[46] that "the most severe reaction would be simply to chase the plane away from Soviet territory." The roots of Soviet irrationality appear to be that the Russians "had honestly been confused and panic-stricken about the enemy intruder."[47]

Three dimensions of irrationality emerge in Soviet behavior in this case: non-comprehensive search-and-evaluation, incompatibility with goals, consensus, or outcomes, and inconsistency of statements and/or actions. Dealing first with non-comprehensive search-and-evaluation, "the Soviet air defence command became over-excited when it thought that it was about to catch an American spy plane deep within its territory,"[48] and this excitement inhibited Soviet ability to evaluate the situation systematically. In particular, Soviet decision makers had their vision narrowed by their "mental set, or the well-known human tendency to see what one expects to see"; this limitation was especially severe because of the "malignant" nature of this viewpoint, seeing the United States as "capable of any amount of deviousness or inhumanity."[49] Calvocoressi[50] explains that Soviet decision makers in the Korean airlines incident displayed "a state of mind conditioned by presupposition, minds closed to the need for evidence." He concludes that "no balanced man, confronted by the question whether to shoot down a civilian airliner or not, could conclude that it was expedient to do so without far firmer identification and confirmation of its supposedly illicit mission."[51] Beyond these individual perceptual filters, bureaucratic problems within the Soviet military organization seemed to inhibit systematic search-and-evaluation:

> Out of all this emerges one consensus: the newly reorganized Soviet military command-and-control system operated by rote early that morning and failed to respond to an unusual situation, thus deeply embarrassing top leadership. The panic and confusion among the various command elements, compounded by anxiety over future promotions, made it difficult for those officers (and there were some) who argued for common sense, careful identification, and caution, to prevail. Instead, the system fell apart. . . .[52]

Second, the decision to shoot down the KAL jet may have been incompatible with the prevailing consensus among Soviet policy makers, as well as with their projection of probable outcomes. The lack of consultation with key decision makers may have set the stage for these incompatibilities:

> President Yuri Andropov evidently was not consulted before the deadly missiles were fired. Nor, it seems, was any member of the ruling politburo. The military acted on its own. Indeed, there is an ambiguity in Ogarkov's [military chief of staff in the Soviet Union] remarks which suggests that the aircraft was already destroyed before the general staff in Moscow was informed.[53]

The absence of "political control of events" and the exclusive dominance of military decision makers[54] show that, while the shooting decision may have been fully compatible with overall Soviet goals, it did not necessarily reflect the prevailing opinion within the Soviet government. This possibility seems especially likely because after the incidents there were signs that the Soviet Communist Party leadership was "not happy" with the action and "would like it to be seen as the action of a reflex-conditioned military mind not accustomed to dealing with considerations of diplomacy and world opinion."[55] This irrationality dimension thus underscores the possibility that the daredevil decision cannot be attributed to the Soviet head-of-state or the Soviet government as a whole, but rather only to one group (the military) within the Soviet chain-of-command.

Turning to inconsistency of statements and/or actions, the most blatant example is the five-day delay before the Soviet Union would even admit that it had shot down the Korean jet.[56] Moreover, although Boris Rygenov—a senior Soviet delegate to the ICAO—called the ICAO report "a gross misrepresentation" full of "assumptions" and "bias," he failed to supply any counter-evidence.[57] Another inconsistency occurred between public statements by the Russians insisting that their actions were fully justifiable, and an article by a deputy commander-in-chief of the air force in the January 1984 issue of the Soviet Air Force magazine, which "criticized the conduct of ground officers who 'hide behind the backs of others,' and implicitly condemned the conduct of the SU–15 pilot who shot down the Korean plane."[58] A final inconsistency of Soviet statements occurred when Radio Moscow, contrary to other Soviet explanations of the incident, "went so far as to pick up and wildly distort an Italian newspaper interview" with John Keppel, a retired State Department official: "The Soviet broadcast twisted this into an allegation by Keppel that U.S. officials had ordered the plane blown up by remote control after the fighter attack so that its spy gear could never be recovered."[59]

Outcome of Irrationality Use

Despite the "U.S.-Soviet recriminations, universal outrage, and more than 80 lawsuits"[60] that immediately followed the Korean Airlines incident, the Soviet action proved to be successful in asserting the sovereignty of its airspace. The Americans denied the Soviet airline Aeroflot the right to land in the United States, but afterwards were relatively eager to improve relations with the Soviet Union. It appears unlikely that the Soviet Union will ever pay compensation for the damages involved.[61] Korean Airlines has changed the flight number of its New York-to-Seoul route (from 007 to 017) and altered the route so that the planes fly further from Sakhalin Island. American foreign affairs specialists[62] indicate that the incident in the long-term "did no significant harm to Moscow's power or image abroad" and has "bolstered the Kremlin's reputation as a strong force not to be trifled with." Thus the daredevil move by the Soviets stunned the world community and at the same time handcuffed adversaries' attempts to take any punitive action.

THE GRENADA INVASION

The origins of the Grenada invasion occurred after Grenada became independent on February 7, 1974. A coalition developed between the New Jewel Movement and other opposition groups against the corrupt Prime Minister Sir Eric Gairy, who employed armed police known as the "Mongoose Gang" to repress disruptions. On March 13, 1979, the New Jewel Movement launched a successful coup d'état against Gairy while he was out of the country, and Maurice Bishop became Prime Minister.

Although the New Jewel Movement began largely as a nationalist group in 1973, after assuming power in Grenada it strengthened its ties to Cuba and the Soviet Union and created a People's Revolutionary Government. The Grenadian "marriage" with the Soviet bloc meant alignment with Moscow "on every international issue," including Afghanistan; the arrival of aid teams from the Soviet Union, Eastern Europe, Libya, Iraq, and North Korea; and the "close friendship" between Bishop and Fidel Castro.[63] Internally, Grenada exhibited a "Marxist-Leninist ruling party, complete with Central Committee and Politburo," a highly developed propaganda machine, and a stringent internal security apparatus.[64]

By 1983 frictions were growing within the New Jewel Movement between Bishop and Deputy Prime Minister Bernard Coard (and his wife Phyllis who controlled Radio Free Grenada). Bishop had become increasingly independent of the Central Committee, due to his stature as an international statesman, and this tendency created frustration within the committee, which supported the principle of "collective leadership."[65] In September 1983 the Central Committee approved the "joint leadership" of Bishop and Coard, but Bishop considered this more of a demonstration of "no confidence" and boycotted most of the meetings that month.[66] After a largely economic mission to Czechoslovakia, Hungary, the Soviet Union, East Berlin, and Cuba from September 27th to October 8th, Bishop returned to Grenada and began circulating the rumor that Coard was plotting Bishop's assassination. The Central Committee launched an investigation, traced the rumor back to Bishop, and then dismissed him from the party and placed him under house arrest on October 14th.

On October 19th a crowd of three thousand led by Bishop's supporters marched to Bishop's home and freed him. The group then marched to army headquarters at Fort Rupert and disarmed the garrison. A few hours later troops from the People's Revolutionary Army arrived, led by Major Leon Cornwall (the former ambassador to Cuba), and fired into the crowd. The PRA then dispersed the crowd and executed Bishop and his most trusted followers. At that point General Hudson Austin, chief of the PRA, dismissed the Central Committee and created the Revolutionary Military Council. The RMC imposed a curfew, closed the airport, and sanctioned multiple arrests, while the Grenadians were in an uproar over Bishop's execution and the new restrictions and engaged in rioting and looting.

The United States had considered the New Jewel Movement government to be destabilizing soon after its inception, but the Senate Intelligence Committee had ordered the CIA in July 1981 to refrain from direct political action there.[67] Afterwards the United States relied more on "massive spying techniques using aerial photography" and on intimidating large-scale naval exercises close to Grenada from 1981 to 1983.[68] The chaos following Bishop's assassination seemed to provide an excellent opportunity for intervention.

The American invasion of Grenada was ostensibly in response to a formal request on October 23rd from the Organization of Eastern Caribbean States for assistance to deal with the "anarchic conditions," "violations of human rights," and "unprecedented threat to the peace and security of the region"; as well as in response to a confidential appeal from Sir Paul Scoon, Governor-General of Grenada, to the OECS to restore order to the island.[69] On October 25, 1983 a combined American-Caribbean security force invaded

Grenada. This force included troops from Barbados, Jamaica, and four members of the OECS in addition to American troops, but the United States provided air, sea, and mechanized support for the operation. After only a few days of fighting, the force accomplished all of its major military objectives by October 28th. The casualty figures were small:[70] for Americans, eighteen killed in action and one hundred and sixteen wounded; for Grenadians, forty-five killed and 1,337 wounded; and for Cubans on the island, twenty-four killed and fifty-nine wounded. The evacuation of almost six hundred American citizens occurred without incident. By December 15th, the United States withdrew its last combat troops from the island, leaving only training, police, medical, and support personnel, and commenced a continuous program of massive economic assistance to the island to improve the stability there.

United States' Goals and Strategies

American goals and motives in the Grenada invasion are complex and reflect considerable controversy. Even the definition of the United States action is the subject of debate, as Ambassador Jeane Kirkpatrick asserted that it was not an "invasion" but rather a "rescue."[71] In President Reagan's letter of explanation to Congress on October 25th and in the State Department's published statement of the American position, the basic reasons for the action were (1) "to ensure the safety of approximately 1000 U.S. citizens whose lives were endangered by the breakdown of law and order, by a shoot-on-sight curfew, and by an unpredictable internal power struggle"; and (2) "to respond to a formal request for assistance" from the OECS and Governor-General Scoon.[72] While the United States contended that these motives provided the legal and moral basis for intervention, some analysts found them to be the "flimsiest" justification and a "mere excuse" for intervention due to the scanty evidence that American nationals "were in any peril"[73] and to the possibility that the United States government manipulated the initiation of the OECS and Scoon requests.[74] President Reagan himself later justified American action on the basis of pursuing a rather different goal—to counter "a Cuban-Soviet plot to render Grenada as a base and 'colony' "[75]—but this motive was again suspect due to the "credibility" problem concerning American estimates of Soviet and Cuban involvement.[76] Other motivations for the invasion of Grenada may have been to free the Grenadians from dictatorship by "thugs," as Reagan called them,[77] and "to install a friendly government" with democratic rule.[78] Perhaps the most cynical and telling explanation of the American invasion has nothing to do with the circumstances in Grenada and instead rests on the American need to demonstrate its military might, or "to win one somewhere,"[79] especially given the major defeat the United States had recently suffered in Lebanon. Not to act during the Grenada crisis, Reagan Administration officials stated at the time, "would have made the United States seem a 'paper tiger'."[80]

The strategy used by the United States to pursue these objectives incorporated political, military, and economic elements. The political moves involved gaining and maintaining regional approval through the OECS for American action toward Grenada, and issuing propaganda during and after the confrontation to demonstrate the level of communist interference in Grenada and the dire need for American action. The primary military move was the invasion itself. The economic moves included the Agency for International Development flying to Grenada emergency supplies valued at $475,000 as soon as the fighting stopped, and a Congressionally approved fifteen-million-dollar package to stimulate long-term economic development in Grenada.[81]

United States' Irrationality

The American invasion of Grenada exemplified daredevil irrationality. Confronted with a presumed communist threat to the region and an internal threat to Americans living in Grenada, the United States overreacted by launching an all-out war against a tiny island. While a show-of-force might have been expected, an actual invasion was a rash move. The action appeared to have violated the principles of international law[82] and international order[83] purportedly in order to uphold law and order. The move developed so rapidly and unexpectedly that President Reagan did not even have time to consult with Prime Minister Thatcher, his close ally with major British interests in the Caribbean: she "learned of the decision to invade only after the action was under way, and immediately expressed strong reservations."[84]

The principal dimensions of irrationality displayed by the United States in the Grenada episode are inconsistency of statements and/or actions and non-comprehensive search-and-evaluation. The first dimension of inconsistency is best demonstrated by the differing, and potentially conflicting, motivations discussed earlier, incorporating deception that seemed probably intentional. Given the military scale of the American action in Grenada, it is quite difficult to believe that it was even initially intended to be simply a rescue mission of American civilians there (as Reagan claimed). Furthermore, since most of the more convincing evidence of Cuban and Soviet influence in Grenada emerged only after the invasion,[85] it is hard to accept that the Reagan Administration believed its own rhetoric about an imminent major Cuban-Soviet plot there. Perhaps the most vivid case of alleged deception concerns the circumstances surrounding the invitation for the United States to intervene in Grenada:

> It is now clear that the United States approached Barbados and the OECS states (less Grenada) on the possibility of intervention rather than the other way around, as the OECS chairman, Eugenia Charles, insisted. The OECS justified its intervention on the basis of an extraordinary interpretation of Article 8 of the OECS treaty dealing with defense against external aggression. Adams [Prime Minister of Barbados] said that the US approach had been made on 15 October, that the request for help by the Governor-General, Sir Paul Scoon, had been written on board USS *Guam* and delivered to him by a Barbadian brigadier. . . .[86]

These revelations, if accurate, would certainly alter the justifiability of the American action.

The demonstration of the non-comprehensive search-and-evaluation by American decision makers is equally direct. In several aspects of the Grenada episode, American claims turned out to be wrong due to a lack of needed information or analysis. A key example was the new airport facility under construction at Port Salines and scheduled for completion in March 1984. President

Reagan concluded that "in a sea of splashing dominoes" the 9,800-foot runway was "excessive" and that it must have been intended for use by Soviet and Cuban air forces and as a base for shipping arms to Nicaragua.[87] But there was considerable "contrary evidence":[88] "British engineers who designed the airport insisted they had done so to civilian specifications and that there were none of the special facilities needed for military use," and the Nicaraguan concern "made no sense geographically." The airport had been planned as early as 1926 by the British strictly to permit development of the tourist industry.[89] In a related matter, the initial American claim that there were 1,500 Cubans in Grenada was deemed by at least one analyst[90] to be "wildly inaccurate." The controversial exclusion of the news media from Grenada during the first two days of the invasion increased the questioning of the credibility of the Reagan Administration's assertions[91] and reduced the availability of contrary information for policy makers. Finally, the previously mentioned lack of consultation with key interested allies such as Britain impeded sound decision making.

Outcome of Irrationality Use

While the American invasion of Grenada may have offended its European allies and removed the United States from "the moral high ground," the action was successful in attaining American objectives. As Dickey[92] points out, "With minimum casualties and an enormous outpouring of popular support back home, the U.S. armed forces achieved all three goals set for them in the invasion order" (protecting American citizens, restoring order and democratic rule, and eliminating Cuban intervention in the island). A CBS News Poll conducted on November 3, 1983 indicated that ninety-one percent of the Grenadians were "glad the United States troops came."[93] Despite an uncertain political future and an unstable economy, nine months after the invasion the American presence seemed "still popular."[94] Cuba's influence throughout the Caribbean has "been considerably set back":[95] "not only had Cuba to warn Nicaragua that it could not give assistance adequate enough to counter a full-scale US invasion but it was forced virtually to close its important embassy in Suriname on the orders of the apprehensive military junta." The daredevil approach by the United States in Grenada has set a precedent of unpredictable threat in the entire Caribbean, giving the United States through fear if not trust the hegemony it has so long sought over at least some of its southern neighbors.

SYNTHESIS

This chapter's three cases all involve aggressive action by the initiating state within its sphere of influence in order simultaneously to protect its citizens from interference by foreigners and to enhance the image of power and legitimacy of the national regime and its policies. Iran took over the American embassy to rid itself of, and extract concessions from, negative Western influence, and to establish the pre-eminence of the Khomeini regime; the Soviet Union shot down the Korean Airlines jet to keep its airspace from foreign intrusion and to demonstrate its resolve and capabilities in this regard; and the United States militarily invaded Grenada to protect its citizens there from the prevailing chaos and communist influence and to demonstrate its military might in the Caribbean and Central America. Because each of these cases could at least be couched in terms of protecting the interests of the initiating state's own citizens, internal and international reactions are somewhat more muted than they might have been otherwise.

In the three cases the specific nature of the aggressive action encompassed a surprising, violent, speedy, military move, completed while the initiating state retained a significant local power advantage, and the daredevil irrationality removed opponents' bargaining chips and handcuffed adversaries' ability to take effective counter-actions In the Iranian hostage confrontation the United States was completely unprepared for the embassy takeover and found itself with no way to negotiate effectively or free the hostages through direct action; in the Korean Airlines confrontation neither Korea nor the United States could exact reparations from the Russians or even induce them to admit guilt; and in the Grenada confrontation nobody was even in a position to reprimand, negotiate with, or oust the American troops after they took over the island. This lack of preparation by the target, combined with the quick, decisive nature of the initiator's military move, created maximum vulnerability to daredevil irrationality.

In comparatively evaluating the success of the three cases, it appears that such applications of daredevil irrationality are more effective if they occur within the initiator's own territory, as in the Iranian hostage and Korean Airlines confrontations, rather than outside of this territory, as in the case of the Grenada invasion. The reasoning here is that the potential for retaliation and counteraction is much lower when one's aggressive action takes place within one's own boundaries.

In all three of the cases the initiators' goals either changed or were ambiguous or controversial during the confrontations, but for daredevil irrationality—unlike stick-in-the-mud irrationality—this wavering of purpose did not inhibit effectiveness due to the premium placed on unpredictability in the daredevil approach. Although the initiating state used a compellent strategy overturning the status quo in the Iran hostages and Grenada invasion cases and a deterrent strategy reinforcing the status quo in the Korean Airlines case, these distinctions do not seem to have had as great an impact on the effectiveness of daredevil irrationality as they did on that on the stick-in-the-mud variety.

6.

"Daredevil" Irrationality—
Failures

The final set of case studies display daredevil irrationality and
largely fail to achieve their objectives. The scrutinized cases are
Iraq's role in the Iran-Iraq War, Argentina's initiation of the Falkland Islands War, and Libya's attack from its embassy in Britain.
All three cases involve the initiation of violence without anticipation
of the scope and dire nature of such action.

THE IRAN-IRAQ WAR

The Iran-Iraq dispute traces back to the rivalry between the Persian and Ottoman empires in the sixteenth century.[1] The disagreements have traditionally focused on border disputes around the
Shatt al-Arab river, which forms the southern boundary between
Iran and Iraq. In the twentieth century, border incidents and propaganda warfare continued between the two nations. In the early
1970's, the Iraqi army focused its attention on the Kurdish rebellion
in the northeastern region, a drive for self-autonomy which Iran
extensively supplied with weapons and logistical support. But on
March 6, 1975 President Saddam Hussein of Iraq and the Shah of
Iran met in Algiers and agreed to a treaty specifying that Iran would
cease its support for the Kurdish rebellion, that adjustments which
were favorable to Iran would occur in the boundary between the
states, and that the two states would halt their mutual propaganda
war.[2] A sign of the temporary thaw in Iran-Iraq relations was Iraq's

compliance with Iran's request in October 1978 to expel Ayatollah Khomeini from Iraq, where he had lived in exile from Iran since 1964.

In February 1979 the Iraqi government "welcomed the Khomeini revolution,"[3] but the relations between Iraq and Iran deteriorated later that year when the Khomeini regime made clear its desire to export Islamic revolution to Iraq, whose "Sunni-dominated regime was preaching a secular ideology to a country with a large Shi'ite population,"[4] as well as to other Arab states. Hussein's secular nationalism inherently clashed with Khomeini's messianic universalism.[5] In October 1979 President Hussein criticized Iran for its expansionist designs on Bahrain and Kuwait. After attacks by Iranian Revolutionary Guards on the Iraqi embassy and on Iraqi consulates in Iran, negotiations ceased between the two nations, and border incidents escalated. In the first half of 1980, "Iraq and Iran launched cross-border raids, artillery duels, aerial dogfights, and political assassination attempts against each other."[6]

Iraq at this point "calculated that in military terms Iran was weaker locally and more isolated internationally than had ever been the case before,"[7] and Iraq received the "stamp of approval" for invasion from Saudi Arabia, Jordan, and the smaller Gulf states, who expected "a quick and favorable outcome."[8] So in September 1980 Iraq invaded Iran. Iraq's incursions began on September 9th, but after some initial advances the Iraqi drive stalled by the end of the first six weeks of the war. On September 22nd the conflict had erupted into a full-scale war, with both sides attacking each other's territory with planes and heavy artillery. A period of stalemate ensued in December, after which—by summer 1982—Iran was able to repel the Iraqis from most of the Iranian territory they had occupied. The major Iranian offensives against Iraq in Iraqi territory, in the summer and early fall, were also unsuccessful, largely due to Iraq's superior weaponry. Since spring 1983, the war "has become one of attrition, with both sides unable to make progress on the ground."[9] While the threat of closure of the Persian Gulf in 1983 and the actual strikes and counter-strikes on shipping in 1984 heightened Western concern about the conflict,[10] these new developments did not increase the chances of war termination. Iraq in 1984 even used mustard gas and other outlawed toxic chemical weapons to break the impasse, but to no avail. Total casualties on both sides in mid–1985 exceeded 280,000 killed (estimates have gone up to a million dead) and more than 760,000 wounded, missing in action, or taken prisoner,[11] along with severe and widespread property damage. The war has created over a million refugees and has cost the participants "billions of dollars in lost resources and revenues."[12] For Iraq, the war has been costing over five hundred million dollars a month.[13]

Outside efforts to mediate the Iran-Iraq War have not succeeded so far. The UN Security Council has called on both sides to stop fighting and to accept a cease-fire. In addition, the Organization of the Islamic Conference, the Nonaligned Movement, and the Gulf Cooperation Council have attempted to mediate, and Turkey, India, and Algeria have offered their services as third-party mediators.[14] Despite the involvement of the high-stakes oil issue, the Soviet and American responses have been "surprisingly cautious and reserved" to the war, and neither side has seen a particular advantage for the other in the conflict,[15] although the United States had up until very recently "gradually abandoned its policy of neutrality and non-involvement in favor of a 'tilt' toward Iraq."[16] The mediation efforts are stymied largely not by Iraq, which "would agree to a step-by-step withdrawal from Iran," but by Khomeini, who has rejected "accepting premature compromises with a badly wounded, vulnerable and yet satanic, foe,"[17] has insisted that Iraq pay substantial reparations to Iran, and has even demanded that Hussein be removed as Iraq's leader.[18] Occasionally there has been some[19] "accumulating evidence of sharp differences among Iran's leaders over military strategy, and some sign that Tehran may be moderating its war objectives," but too conciliatory a strategy would seem "out of character" for Khomeini.

Iraq's Goals and Strategies

Iraq's precise objectives in the war are somewhat "obscure"[20]—"there remains a fundamental doubt as to what Iraqi objectives may have been, or may now become."[21] Despite the ambiguity, certain goals do seem to emerge with regularity. Hussein's territorial ends, which do not appear to have been the fundamental driving force behind the invasion, included regaining not only the border area lost to Iran in the 1975 Algiers Treaty, but also Arabistan (also called Khuzistan)—the home of Iran's Arab minority.[22] Another objective motivating the invasion was to restore domestic stability within Iraq:

> The Iraqi regime itself was unstable, the product of a dozen conspiracies, and its taste for internal bloodletting was infamous even by local standards. . . . Moreover, there were permanent sources of discord within the Iraqi state. . . . The appeal of the Ayatollah Khomeini for a rising of Iraqi Shi'ites against the Sunnis of Baghdad found followers. Thus, Saddam Husain's attack on Iran was an act of internal repression as well as international aggression.[23]

A third goal was Iraq's "quest for leadership" in the Persian Gulf area[24]—"an ambitious man, Saddam Hussein was seeking to have Iraq replace Iran as the preponderant power in the Gulf and to replace Egypt . . . as the leader of the Arab world."[25] If Iraq defeated Iran, then "there would be no real contesting Hussein's preeminence among Arabs, and the Arab world would have a new and far more successful Nasser."[26] However, as the conflict progressed, Iraq realized that Iran's defeat was not imminent, and the Iraqi goals became more modest—"to agree to a cease-fire, and then to bargain for territorial concessions."[27]

Iraq's military strategy to achieve these objectives has been described as "tortuous."[28] Initially its war plan was "to destroy Iran's oil sources, refineries and transportation routes, and by cutting these off from the rest of the country to put the political regime in Tehran in a vise from which neither it nor the Iranian people could break free."[29] Anxious to avoid heavy casualties, the Iraqi army has emphasized artillery barrage rather than frontal infantry assaults, followed by cautious advances of tanks and personnel carriers.[30] Neither side has totally committed its forces, instead preferring "9-to–5 artillery exchanges, occasional air sorties, and rare naval action."[31] In the process, the Iraqi army has "sought to minimize close contact with Iranian regulars" and rather to focus on Khomeini's Revolutionary Guards as the target.[32] The Iraqis "have a decided advantage in air power, in the quantity and quality of their arms and equipment, and in being able to shift forces rapidly owing to the better network of roads behind their own lines"; but Iran has superiority in raw manpower, resulting in the use of the "human wave" battlefield tactic, with a population nearly three times as large as Iraq's.[33]

Iraq's Irrationality

Iraq's decision to invade Iran exhibits daredevil irrationality. The idea of a swift, decisive, shocking attack as a means of redressing grievances against Iran and of taking advantage of Iranian vulnerability seems to be a rash and overreactive policy to cope with the instability and threat posed by a hostile Khomeini government. Wright[34] calls this Iraqi daredevil approach "the classic Clausewitzian design"—"an extension of the politics of border negotiations by means of a military seige"—attempting to communicate credible resolve through willingness to undertake unexpectedly costly and committing actions in the course of the dispute.

Iraq's decisions in the Iran-Iraq War display both non-comprehensive search-and-evaluation and inconsistency of statements and/ or actions. The non-comprehensive search-and-evaluation occurred most significantly in Iraq's miscalculation about expecting a "swift and decisive" victory in the war.[35] Cottam best describes the exact nature of this "mistake of truly historic proportions," which was heavily laced with wishful thinking:

> In May, 1980, Tareq Aziz, Deputy Prime Minister of Iraq, gave a speech in which he described conditions in Iran. The picture he painted was one of military weakness, an economy near collapse, internal anarchy, and a foreign policy in shambles....
>
> Military analysts tend after the fact to denigrate the training, the leadership and the strategy of the Iraqi military. But the real miscalculation was political. Confident that the picture of Iran painted by Aziz was accurate, Hussein believed Iran would collapse into an anarchic situation that could easily lead to the disintegration of the state. The Iraqi military staff thus did not need to engage in the kind of preparation that led to the early brilliant victories of the Egyptian military in

1973. Rather, a fairly modest move should have produced the desired political results.[36]

What Hussein ignored, as it turned out, was "the patriotic zeal of the Iranian people, who set aside much of their chaotic internal strife once the war erupted to rally behind the cause of rescuing their country."[37] Iraq's "serious miscalculations about the loyalty and cohesiveness of their adversary's population" seemed to be "errors that flow naturally from the attitudes of cultural condescension that are endemic to the Middle East."[38]

Iraq's inconsistency of statements and/or actions is somewhat reflected just in the murkiness of its goals. But a couple of specific contradictory examples stand out. First, Wright illustrates hypocrisy concerning territorial claims:

> Before the war, Minister Hammadi, when asked (by this writer) whether any part of Khuzistan was claimed as Iraqi territory, responded, 'We have no territorial claims in Iran.' Similar statements were made in October by top Iraqi officials, but by the end of the month First Deputy President Taha Yasin Ramadan, asked what would become of Iran's oil once Iraqi forces had captured Abadan and the surrounding region, responded:"It will become Iraqi oil until a solution is found. Arabistan's oil will be Iraqi as long as Tehran refuses to negotiate.'[39]

Second, Iraq has displayed indignation at the charge that it has used mustard gas against Iran during the war, but "it has never directly refuted the charges that it has used chemical weapons in the conflict,"[40] and in March 1984 the United Nations confirmed that Iraq not only used mustard gas but tear gas as well.

Outcome of Irrationality Use

While the Iran-Iraq War does not seem to be close to a decisive military outcome, it is readily apparent that Iraq's invasion failed to achieve its goals. Even its modest desire for a cease-fire has seemed unattainable; Iraq has been "denied success even for its most minimal military objectives."[41] As Claiborne[42] points out, the outcome of the clash between Iraq and Iran "will be determined not on the battlefield in the classic military sense, but by how long the two countries can sustain their supply lines to the front and on how willing they are to continue fighting in the face of inevitable economic hardships at home." The economic cost to Iraq has indeed been high—the country's port has been closed and oil production has plummeted.[43] In this respect, Iraq may be at a disadvantage:

> Unable to move oil through the Gulf or through a pipeline in hostile Syria, the Iraqi regime is becoming increasingly dependent on financial assistance from Arab allies. And, because of the state of the oil market, that assistance has been reduced. As a result, the Iraqi population is increasingly feeling the effects of the war.[44]

Thus in Baghdad "a mood of despair and disillusionment now permeates the capital, as an eroding economy and the futile war erase visions of a strong and prosperous Iraq that would dominate the oil-exporting region in the 1980's."[45] To add insult to injury, "evidence mounted that the Khomeini regime would be strengthened by the attack,"[46] for the Iranian government "has consolidated its position and the internal threat for the time being has receded."[47] Due to Iran's intractability, "the prospects for any negotiated settlement seem utterly remote."[48] The trends in the war continue to fluctuate:[49] in 1984 some contended that there had been increased Iraqi support for their government, some stabilization in the Iraqi economy, an improved Iraqi military position, and greater international political support, but later on observers switched their position and felt Iran possessed the advantage; in any case, even optimistic views accept the probability that "the drain on Iraq's manpower and the strain on its economy could sooner or later weaken the will of the population to continue the war." Iraq's daredevil mistake has helped to create a rather dismal future.

THE FALKLAND ISLANDS WAR

The conflict over the Falkland Islands, which was "the first real naval war since 1945,"[50] had "great symbolic importance" despite the "little intrinsic significance" of the Falklands to the United Kingdom or Argentina.[51] Argentine administration of the Falkland Islands had originated in 1829. The United States and Britain later protested the Argentine seizure of three American fishing vessels allegedly violating fishing regulations in the area and, when there was no Argentine response, Britain took over by force the Falklands in January 1833 and expelled the Argentine soldiers and settlers.[52] British occupation and administration of the Falklands continued undisturbed until 1982, although Argentina had asserted claims to these islands "by means of protest notes, which were loftily ignored by the British Foreign Office."[53]

After World War II, when President Péron first assumed power in Argentina, "these dispersed assertions of the Argentine claim were merely mentioned more often, official thinking still being that the 'Malvinas' would eventually be Argentine."[54] Although very minor clashes occurred between Argentina and Britain over control of the Falklands in 1952, 1966, and 1975, "contemplation of the use of force has not been a permanent feature of the approach of the various very different Argentine political regimes to the dispute in the South Atlantic."[55] However, "it was under the military regime from 1976 onwards that the change took place and commentators began indicating that spectacular and unprecedented action in the 'Malvinas' could be expected to rid the regime of its political and economic embarrassments:"[56] the military regime, under General Leopoldo Galtieri since December 1981, had "repressed guerrilla activity and simultaneously embarked on economic policies which multiplied the foreign debt by a factor of four, reduced the purchasing power of the salaried and wage-earning sectors by 40 percent, abolished tariffs, and allowed interest rates to reach ruinous levels." As Purcell[57] points out, "The taking of the Falklands, given the nationalist surge it would produce, seemed a made-to-order solution" to the Argentine public's dissatisfaction not only with the economy but also with the political corruption and military repression.

On April 2, 1982 Argentina invaded the Falkland Islands with the intent of taking them by force. The British marines there were in no position to resist and soon surrendered. The British government, despite increasingly unambiguous signals from Argentina and confirmation from American intelligence,[58] had not anticipated the invasion. Immediately following the attack, Prime Minister Margaret Thatcher declared that the Royal Navy would retake the Falklands, in response to what Foreign Secretary Lord Carrington described as a "national humiliation,"[59] and sent a thirty-five-ship task force to the South Atlantic. On April 12th, Britain declared a maritime exclusion zone two hundred miles around the Falklands. But the British fleet took nearly three weeks to travel the eight thousand miles to its target destination, which it reached on April 30th, presumably in order to allow time for a diplomatic solution to develop.[60]

Prior to the outbreak of the actual fighting numerous outside mediation attempts occurred. On April 3rd, the United Nations Security Council requested that all forces withdraw, that hostilities cease, and that British-Argentine negotiations begin. Several days later the Common Market imposed economic sanctions on Argentina. The Organization of American States passed resolutions supporting Argentina's territorial claims and condemning Britain's armed attack on the Falklands. The "most ambitious and spectacular attempt to avoid military conflict between Britain and Argentina was the long-distance shuttle diplomacy of U.S. Secretary of State Alexander M. Haig, Jr.";[61] the United States on April 30th ultimately ended up siding with the British and provided some aid to them while imposing limited economic sanctions on Argentina. All of the efforts to avoid war were to no avail, at least in part because Argentina "insisted that the sovereignty issue be resolved in Argentina's favor *prior* to any negotiations," while "the whole point of negotiations" for Britain "was to resolve disputed sovereignty claims."[62]

At the time of the British assault, "about 10,000 Argentine troops were in place, and their equipment was at least the equal of the British."[63] The first British warships to arrive at the Falklands were nuclear submarines, which sank an Argentine cruiser on May 2nd. A traditional air-sea battle ensued after the British surface fleet arrived later, with much heavier casualties and equipment damage suffered by Argentina than by Britain. Although the British never eliminated Argentine air capabilities, which proved to be the primary Argentine threat, the British fleet began its troop landing on May 21st. The military casualties—eight hundred to one thousand Argentine and two hundred fifty British deaths—were significant but "only a small proportion of the forces committed."[64] On June 14th the Argentine forces surrendered, but "Argentina was literally unable to agree to peace terms, because its new government, after the dismissal of General Galtieri, was far too weak to make so unpopular an announcement, or, for that matter, to guarantee that no successor government would repudiate it."[65]

Argentina's Goals and Strategies

As previously suggested, the central objective of the Argentine invasion of the Falkland Islands was to increase the level of domestic support for the government. The military felt that such an action would "bolster their sagging popularity and thereby set the terms for the transition to civilian rule that might prove necessary":[66] "as late as 30 March, there were vociferous public demonstrations in Argentina against the Junta's economic policies, and it was only the invasion which turned anti-government demonstrations into highly jingoistic anti-British protests."[67] Apparently the Falklands crisis was not the first opportunity that Argentina had used to pursue this diversionary goal:

> The Argentine economy has been a shambles for years, and by the spring of 1982 the military junta ruling the country badly needed an issue that would deflect popular attention from the disastrous state of the economy. It appears first to have sought a confrontation with Chile over the disputed islands in the Beagle Strait (a dispute that almost brought both countries to war in 1978). When Chile failed to rise to the occasion, the Falklands were seized.[68]

In invading the Falkland Islands, Argentina felt that it could expect to gain great support both internally and externally from other Latin American nations, because "for the Latins, Great Britain's control of the Falklands was anachronistic and illegitimate in an age of decolonization."[69] Other possible goals pursued by Argentina—such as access to rumored undersea oil around the Falklands, extension of Antarctic territorial claims, and following the lead of the Argentine scrap metal merchants who raised the Argentine flag on the Falklands on March 19th[70]—appear to have been secondary in Argentine calculations.

The Argentine strategy of invading and taking over the Falklands rested on a number of premises. First, the military regime accepted the idea of "a quick decisive *fait accompli*," to a great extent due to a past history of "the British willingness to negotiate" and "reluctance to take serious measures to defend the Falklands."[71] Second, the Argentine government "believed that the United States would not oppose an Argentine invasion of the Falklands"; and "with the United States out of the picture, and the advantage of geography on their side, the military believed they could defeat any attempt by Britain to recapture the islands."[72] Third, Argentina felt that keeping the action secret, implemented to such an extent that even "the troops en route to the Falklands were not told of their destination," would "reduce any chance for internal criticism of the operation" as well as increase the chances of its success.[73]

Argentina's Irrationality

The Argentine decision to capture the Falkland Islands exhibited characteristics of daredevil irrationality. Given the frustration of a century and a half of British rule of the islands and the growing domestic turmoil, launching an all-out invasion seems to be a rash and reckless overreaction. The Argentine leaders, through cognitive closure and wishful thinking, were overconfident about the likelihood of success for such a venture, and this fearless attitude appeared to be pervasive even among Argentine pilots:

> . . . . at the beginning of World War II, air defenses in general were in so poor a state that the daredevil aspect of early operations was not evident. In the Falklands it was; pilots were indeed willing to take appalling levels of casualties until, one assumes, only the less adventurous ones were left among the living.[74]

This daredevil bravado by leaders and followers seemed almost incomprehensible to many Western observers.

The three specific dimensions of irrationality displayed by Ar-

gentine policy makers were non-comprehensive search-and-evaluation, incompatibility of decisions with goals, consensus, or outcomes, and non-dispassionate style of decision. The non-
comprehensive nature of Argentina's search-and-evaluation comes
to light through a series of Argentine miscalculations, most notable
of which was the belief that "there would be little or no reaction
from Britain":[75] a report of the Argentine Army Commission, established after the war to investigate "what went wrong," concluded
that the invasion was "conceived and executed in an absolutely false
framework." Freedman[76] identifies the key miscalculation involved
as the "underestimation not so much of British anger and readiness
to take up the challenge as of its actual capacity to retake the islands
by military means." This inability of the ruling junta in Argentina
"to form a realistic estimate of the consequences of its operation or
of the British reaction" may associate with the presence of "enormous self-deception both within the junta and through its propaganda organs."[77] Purcell explains that the primary reason for this
miscalculation may have been the Argentine generals' "insularity":

> Accustomed mainly to their version of strategic military think-
> ing, the generals decided the islands lacked strategic impor-
> tance for Britain. They apparently did not take into account
> the role that British domestic pressures and the 'end of Empire'
> psychology would play in determining the British response.
> Moreover, the generals' error in judgment also grew out of
> their belief that the United States, acting under principles dat-
> ing from the Monroe Doctrine and reiterated in the Rio Pact
> (the Inter-American Treaty of Reciprocal Assistance) would
> do everything in its power to prevent European ships from
> entering and doing battle in hemispheric waters.[78]

This lack of systematic evaluation and judgment also surfaced in
the general ineptitude of the Argentine army—selection of officers
may have been the product of "bureaucratic politics," based more
on "loyalty to the ruling junta than on any demonstrated capability," leading to accusations of "incompetence and even
corruption."[79]

This bureaucratic politics also highlighted the incompatibility of
Argentina's decisions and actions with its goals in the war. The

significant "interservice rivalry" among the army, navy, and air-force, along with rivalry between regulars and conscripts, made Argentine forces "unable or at least unwilling to coordinate their operations," and resulted in a striking "inability to make command decisions."[80] Quality policies could not emerge from this process; for example, Argentina could not coordinate air strikes and ground counter-attacks. The poor performance of the Argentine military during the war thus reflected tactical decisions made not on the basis of what was best for the nation or what would best serve its goals, but rather on the basis of the political product of the self-interested squabbling among the three military services acting as "the political powers in a coalition system."[81]

Turning to Argentina's non-dispassionate style of decision, Friedman[82] contends that in its Falkland Islands invasion "the central issue was emotional." This emotionalism was largely a consequence of "the prevailing 'Nuremberg mentality' among Argentine officers"—"they feared for their careers, giving the political weight of the human rights lobby and the calls for an explanation made by the Church, the political parties and the trade unions."[83] Argentine pride appeared in the "outrage" they expressed when they felt the "British were treating them like a Third World state."[84] The usual spate of emotional language preceded the Argentine invasion: for example, the navy asserted as early as February 1982 that "for 149 years the usurpers have enjoyed nothing but advantages."[85]

Outcome of Irrationality Use

Argentina's invasion of the Falkland Islands clearly failed to achieve its goals. The military failure in capturing the islands created even more internal chaos and dissatisfaction than that preceding the invasion, and Argentina will probably not risk further military confrontation with Britain in the near future. Argentina's inability to attract expected support either from the United States or from several Latin American nations (such as Brazil, Mexico, Colombia, Chile, and Guyana)[86] reflected diminished prestige on the continent. For a nation emphasizing "its sense of superiority over the rest of South America" and driving "to rise from Third World to Second

World status,"[87] this lack of support was indeed a blow. Moreover, British resolve to keep the islands grew as a result of the confrontation, and its victory raised national morale[88] and support for Prime Minister Thatcher. The link between Argentina's daredevil irrationality and these failures seems a direct one, and Argentina's emotional and unsystematic "misperceptions and miscalculations" were even critical in "helping to ensure that mediation attempts by the American Secretary of State . . . and others were unsuccessful"[89] in preventing or reducing the conflict and in aiding Argentina.

THE LIBYAN EMBASSY INCIDENT

Since he came to power in 1969 in a bloodless coup overthrowing the corrupt regime of King Idris, Colonel Moammar Khaddafi has undertaken a program of promoting international terrorism that has stunned the West. But since 1980, when his oil revenues plummeted from twenty-two billion dollars to seven billion dollars due to the oil glut, Khaddafi "has cut back on his terrorist patronage and failed to make good on many of his financial promises."[90] At about the same time, the first evidence emerged of domestic unrest under the Khaddafi regime. In 1979–80 Libyan university students engaged in protest demonstrations in Benghazi and Tripoli, and Libyan military personnel linked to French, American, and Egyptian intelligence plotted at Tobruk to overthrow Khaddafi.[91] In 1980, there was an army mutiny near the Egyptian border, and several hundred soldiers were killed. Khaddafi responded to these signs of turmoil by "revolutionizing" the universities through the establishment of new indoctrination committees and compulsory military training for both male and female students (the Libyan People's Congress eliminated conscription of women in February 1984) and by purging his embassies abroad through the replacement of traditional diplomatic representatives with "people's bureaus" headed by loyal followers.[92] In 1981, President Reagan imposed an embargo on oil imports from Libya and on most American exports to Libya, and as a result "shrinking revenues have brought a shortage of essential foods," while attempts "to stamp out internal dissent have only fanned discontent."[93] In 1982 Khaddafi arrested two hundred university students for protesting forced conscription. The spectrum of discontent in Libya today "ranges from Islamic fundamentalists to students to part of the army."[94]

Faced with this escalating internal turmoil, Khaddafi "raised the spectre of a common enemy abroad—his exiled opponents."[95] From February 1980 onwards, he called for the "liquidation of the enemies of the people and revolution" overseas, and there have been numerous successful and unsuccessful assassination attempts in Western Europe since that time, often with support from local Libyan embassies.[96] These murders have "unified the disparate groups" abroad who oppose Khaddafi, "giving them common fears and martyrs."[97] On January 21, 1984, two gunmen from a probable dissident group called "Al-Burkan" (the Volcano) killed Amar Taggazy, a Libyan representative in Rome. Since that time, an internal debate has raged within the Libyan government on how to respond with force to Libyan dissident movements based in Europe, Egypt, and Sudan, and it has appeared that the advocates of "tough measures" won the debate.[98] On February 16th there was a major reshuffling of key government positions, including the creation of the position of minister of external security to underscore Khaddafi's desire to "crack down on expatriate opponents" of Libya.[99] On February 18th the Khaddafi-backed Libyan Revolutionary Students Force took over the embassy in London and expelled the old diplomats. In March there were several bomb attacks (injuring twenty-six people) on Arab businesses in London and Manchester. Finally, in April Khaddafi ordered at the Fatah University campus in Tripoli the hanging of two Muslim fundamentalist students who refused to accept Khaddafi's ideological and religious teachings.

This last anti-dissident act triggered a political demonstration by about seventy opponents of Khaddafi outside the Libyan embassy in London on April 17, 1984. On that day, without any warning, "an unidentified gunman poked the nose of a submachine gun through the curtains of a second-story window" of the Libyan embassy, "spraying the crowd below with a short burst of bullets."[100] A twenty-five-year-old British policewoman, Yvonne Fletcher, was killed, and ten protesters were wounded. Quickly following this incident, Libya's Revolutionary Guards surrounded the British embassy in Tripoli and threatened retaliation against its twenty-five occupants if British security forces, who had surrounded the Libyan embassy in London, attempted any punitive action against the Libyans there.

Within hours of the shooting, British Home Secretary Leon Brittan activated the cabinet office briefing room—known as COBRA—as a communications center for the crisis. British police set up telephone communications with the Libyan embassy and tried to persuade the thirty occupants to leave. On April 22nd, British Minister of State Richard Luce, who had demanded that the British be allowed to search the Libyan embassy for arms and explosives, announced that Libya's response had been "wholly inadequate," that Britain would immediately break diplomatic relations with Libya, and that all Libyans in the embassy had to leave the country by April 29th.[101] Serving as constraints on British tactics were the 8,500 British citizens working in Libya, the specific concern for the British embassy personnel there, and the rules of the 1961 Vienna convention guaranteeing the Libyans diplomatic immunity. On April 26th, after extensive negotiations, the Libyans indicated they were ready to leave, and subsequently the thirty diplomats and their families flew back to Tripoli. At the same time, British diplomats and their families left Tripoli and safely returned to London.

Libya's Goals and Strategies

Libya's goal in the embassy incident appeared to be to oppose through intimidation the expression of dissident anti-government views by protesters in Britain. As previously indicated, Khaddafi viewed the increasing discontent within Libya to be directly connected with and resulting from external agitators, and perceived that suppression of this overseas agitation was critical to the stability of his regime. Presumably the attack on the dissidents might deter future protest demonstrations.

Khaddafi's strategy to achieve this repression of international protest was to sanction violence and terrorism against the dissidents. The effectiveness of this kind of fear tactic was shown by the unwillingness of the protesters at the Libyan embassy in London to show their faces—they wore scarves to conceal them—and of a much larger group of dissidents both inside and outside Libya to express their unhappiness in any manner. The embassy shootings, then, were simply part of a larger array of approaches, including the hanging of students and the bombing of businesses, to achieve the desired end.

Libya's Irrationality

The Libyan embassy incident demonstrated an extreme form of daredevil irrationality. Displeased with spreading dissident activity at home and abroad, the Libyan decision to shoot peaceful protesters and an unarmed policewoman was a rash, overreactive move. As Laver[102] notes, "Even by the standards of Libya's revolutionary Islamic militancy" the "shooting was an alarming display of international terrorism." One analyst[103] called the act the "most brazen" attack yet by Khaddafi's government, and Home Secretary Brittan declared that "this unprovoked and barbaric onslaught is intolerable."

Although many varieties of irrationality may have been involved in Libya's decisions regarding the embassy violence, the two most documentable dimensions are inconsistency of statements and/or actions and non-dispassionate style of decision. The inconsistency emerges most vividly from an exploration of the question of accountability for the incident. The anti-Khaddafi demonstration had been planned well in advance,[104] and Libya's concern about it was shown by the visit on April 16th of two members of the Libyan embassy staff to the British Foreign Office, demanding that the demonstration "must not be allowed to take place."[105] Meanwhile, an American spy satellite intercepted a telephone call between the Libyan government in Tripoli and its embassy in London, instructing the embassy "not to sit 'passively' " while the anti-Khaddafi demonstration occurred nearby.[106] Reportedly Libya had sent a two-man hit team two weeks before the shooting, and the two had hid in a room on the top floor of the embassy in London.[107] Libyan television was even having the demonstration filmed, and speculation was that "the real purpose of the filming might have been to record what happens to Libyan citizens overseas when they stage a demonstration against the government."[108] Despite this convincing evidence and the multiple confirmations that the shooting came from the embassy, Khaddafi's story was quite different:

> Interviewed on NBC TV, the Libyan strong man accused the British police and demonstrators of launching an unprovoked attack on the London embassy. Then, commenting on the death of policewoman Fletcher, he declared, "British police shot themselves."[109]

The Libyan government "kept up a propaganda barrage, accusing Britain of collusion with the U.S. in an effort to damage the reputation" of the Khaddafi regime, and a government-controlled newspaper charged Britain with "setting criminals, the police, and stray dogs onto the Libyan students" at the embassy.[110] This inconsistency of statements and actions seems quite typical of Khaddafi's regime: "The very unpredictability of his actions is what keeps his neighbors off balance and gives him maneuverability . . . there is no real defense against him, because the lengths he is willing to go are so extreme."[111]

The non-dispassionate style of decision is most characteristic of Khaddafi himself. Analysts alternatively describe his personality as "volatile," "petulant," "truly scary," "impulsive," or "paranoid" and view him as "an eccentric planner of havoc" or as "a sick terrorist" obsessed with "satanic games."[112] Khaddafi is clearly one of the most emotional and mercurial leaders of our times. The debate seems to be only over the source of the emotionalism, as the Bishop of Salisbury indicated at the funeral service for the slain British policewoman: "As each new act of corruption is reported, we slip too easily into saying of the perpetrators, 'They must be mad.' But the problem is not madness. It is wickedness."[113] While no doubt such harsh judgments are heavily tainted with Western bias, even President Anwar Sadat of Egypt once said that Khaddafi was "either 100 percent crazy or possessed of the devil."[114] Whatever the nature of Khaddafi's irrationality, Western leaders find it incomprehensible.

Outcome of Irrationality Use

The outcome of the Libyan embassy incident appeared to be failure, even though there is no way to gauge completely its impact on anti-Khaddafi dissident groups. The Khaddafi regime itself seemed to recognize that its strategy had been unsuccessful: "Though the Libyan government publicly maintained what one Western observer in Tripoli described as a 'defiant sulk', the British gradually decided that Khaddafi realized that the shooting incident had damaged Libyan interests and was anxious to get it over with."[115] Laver[116] asserted that Khaddafi's "perversion of diplomatic privilege for his bloody revenge campaign has now fanned international outrage in a way none of his other expansionist provocations have before." The incident led to a rupture of diplomatic relations between Libya and Britain, and Britain and other nations have reconsidered the rules of diplomatic immunity.[117] The Reagan Administration expressed its hope as a result of the incident that its Western allies will take more severe anti-Libya measures.[118] Despite Khaddafi's continued feistiness and support for terrorism in the period following the Libyan embassy incident, no other moves of this type have occurred since. The emotional and deceptive approach of the Libyans appears to have been centrally responsible for preventing a more effective outcome (dissident protest continues) and for producing the antagonistic reactions.

SYNTHESIS

In the three cases in this chapter, the initiating state engaged in violent aggression in order to improve the image of the regime's power and legitimacy internally and externally. Iraq invaded Iran to repress internal dissent and to establish its leadership in the Persian Gulf; Argentina invaded the Falkland Islands to decrease opposition from domestic dissidents and to increase support from other Latin American nations; and Libya initiated the embassy shooting in London to calm internal unrest and to silence international opposition to the regime. Unlike the cases in the previous chapter, the goal of image enhancement could not be convincingly accompanied by that of protecting the initiating state's own citizens; indeed, Iraq, Argentina, and Libya had governmental regimes far more interested in military repression of domestic opposition than in responding to domestic needs. The absence of this link to citizens'

interests proved to be somewhat critical in legitimizing and ex-
panding the range of counter-moves available to the target nations.

While daredevil irrationality provided through its unpredictability a temporary aggressive advantage for the initiating state in each
case, the nature of the confrontations required more long-term
power advantages which were simply not available. Iraq made significant advances in Iran, but then could not hold on and was largely
repulsed; Argentina initially succeeded in taking over the Falklands,
but then could not withstand the British assault; and Libya managed
to halt the demonstration outside of its London embassy, but then
could not avoid the diplomatic setbacks from the events which
followed the shooting. Unlike the last chapter's daredevil incidents,
where the temporary local power advantage was sufficient to provide a stable and favorable outcome, the three cases here required
a much more continuous and perhaps even semi-permanent advantage for the initiating states to maintain and exploit their momentary
gains. Maintaining control of newly acquired territory, as in the
case of Iraq and Argentina, or causing a terrorist shooting in another
state to benefit one's own image, as in the case of Libya, seems to
be a costly, long-term proposition. Daredevil irrationality seems to
be inherently incapable, due to its dependence on surprise, of producing this kind of semi-permanent advantage.

Closely examining these three daredevil failures indicates that the
target state's relationship to the initiating state's sphere of influence
may be relevant. Unlike the cases in the last chapter, none of the
initiators faced an opponent located within their sphere of influence,
and drifting outside of one's sphere of influence—as is especially
evident in the Iraq and Libya cases—can increase the probability
of retaliation. All three initiating states used compellent strategies
attempting to alter the status quo, and one initiator—Iraq—had
somewhat obscure and fluctuating objectives, but neither of these
qualities seemed to play an important role in causing the use of
daredevil irrationality to be unsuccessful.

7.

Evaluation of Case Study Patterns

The case studies in the preceding chapters reveal several tentative but intriguing patterns about when irrationality is most and least successful in attaining policy goals in international confrontations. This chapter reviews existing claims from the relevant literature about the general utility of irrationality, describes the findings from the case studies, and then compares these claims to these findings. Patterns emerge depicting differences between stick-in-the-mud and daredevil irrationality, as well as among incompatibility of decisions with goals, consensus, or outcomes, non-comprehensive search-and-evaluation, inconsistency of statements and/or actions, and non-dispassionate style of decision. In the process of identifying these differences, this analysis implicitly and explicitly rejects many intuitive assumptions about the desirability of rationality and irrationality.

PREVAILING CONTENTIONS ON THE UTILITY OF IRRATIONALITY

The existing literature is quite general and somewhat vague about the conditions when irrationality is preferable in international relations. This literature rarely distinguishes between the utility of genuine and manipulated irrationality and rarely analyzes the drawbacks of irrationality when it is deemed preferable. Nonetheless, a brief summary of the prevailing wisdom on irrationality provides a useful backdrop for the case study findings.

Irrationality defined as decisions' incompatibility with policy goals, prevailing consensus, or preferred outcomes can be preferable in a couple of broad ways. The most obvious one occurs when the prevailing societal consensus clashes with policy goals and preferred outcomes.[1] Even with a prioritization of the tradeoffs involved, rational decision makers in a responsible pluralistic society may be handcuffed in such a situation, particularly if they consider the views of the people to be rationally unacceptable.[2] Another advantage of irrationality would be if a rational perspective prevented gaining the insights needed to pursue policy goals or preferred outcomes. Frankel[3] explains that "an excess of rationality leads to a lack of understanding," and he uses as an example Konrad Adenauer's rationality preventing him as head-of-state in Germany from understanding stupid or irrational behavior. Beyond these broad benefits, a few more specific differentiations emerge from the literature[4] about the utility of irrationality here: incompatibility with goals seems best when the goals demand an expedient solution violating moral or socio-cultural norms and/or when pursuing the goals has consistently resulted in failure due to their unattainability; incompatibility with consensus seems best when the public or government is inadequately informed and/or when the societal or bureaucratic consensus is motivated by internal political power concerns rather than external policy effectiveness concerns; and incompatibility with outcomes seems best when facing irrational adversaries (whose actions violate the assumptions of the projected outcomes), when having little information, and/or when facing unacceptable demands from a clearly superior state.

Irrationality defined as non-comprehensive search-and-evaluation can frequently be preferable in foreign policy. Turning first to stick-in-the-mud irrationality, many decision theorists[5] believe that incrementalism and satisficing are the most desirable decision processes because of (1) the reduced costs—in terms of time, information, personnel, or other resources—of searching for just a few policy alternatives and (2) the limited and biased human problem-solving capabilities. Stein[6] notes that, especially in crises, these sub-optimizing strategies can prevent policy makers from committing a "great error" and, given advanced military technology, from initiating global disaster. Morgan[7] concurs and calls this irrationality in the deterrence context "sensible" decision making. In routine situations, the costs of being comprehensive may be too large when compared with the smallness of the resulting benefits.[8] As to dare-devil irrationality, Schelling is insightful:

> It is not invariably an advantage, in the face of a threat, to have a communications system in good order, to have complete information, or to be in full command of one's own actions or of one's own assets. . . . The very notion that it may be a strategic advantage to relinquish certain options deliberately, or even to give up all control over one's future actions and make his reactions automatic, seems to be a hard one to swallow.[9]

An irrational state which claims that it has no other choice but to respond in a certain dramatic way may indeed be in an advantageous position. More specifically,[10] stick-in-the-mud non-comprehensive search-and-evaluation seems best when there are time pressures, trivial issues, minor or reversible consequences, scarce decision resources, and/or no past series of paralyzing incremental policies; and daredevil non-comprehensive search-and-evaluation seems best when facing rational states in restrained and/or conciliatory modes.

Irrationality involving inconsistency of statements and/or actions can also be beneficial. Being logically inconsistent over time can help to create a smoke screen of ambiguity, thus keeping several paths open simultaneously and protecting crucial images.[11] A growing number of writers[12] show how strategies of deception and surprise, accomplished through considerable inconsistency, can be successful in achieving foreign policy objectives. George[13] points out that some manifestations of a decision maker's "consistency-striving" are "excessive and possibly harmful in policy making," especially when the beliefs are not initially well grounded (causing valid inferences from invalid premises) or when officials are not sufficiently responsive to contradictory information or opposing arguments. In particular,[14] inconsistency of statements and/or actions may be best when one rarely uses it (to avoid the "boy-who-cried-wolf" syndrome), when one needs to extricate oneself ("decouple") in a face-saving manner from an adverse situation, when one needs surprise or bluff due to an adversary's superiority, when one possesses an image clearly vulnerable to an adversary, and/or when one needs flexibility due to rapidly changing external circumstances.

Finally, irrationality involving non-dispassionate style of decision may be useful. Janis and Mann[15] contend that "the desirability of cool detachment as an ideal is highly questionable. A world dominated by Dr. Strangelove and like-minded cost accountants might soon become devoid of affection, conscience, and humanity, as well as passion." These authors further assert[16] that "obsessive imaginative activity in a state of hypervigilance may have adaptive value ...insofar as it contributes to preparation for coping with unavoidable setbacks that arise later on." Rationality may certainly be more dull and uncreative than irrationality.[17] More specific contentions[18] indicate that stubborn and determined emotions seem best when a nation has a low reputation for resolve and credibility and wants to communicate strong intent, and that kind and caring emotions seem best when international sympathy and external support are critical for a policy's effectiveness.

From the sparse theoretical threads provided by existing contentions concerning irrationality, it appears that irrationality can occasionally be preferable for nations in the initiation of their own foreign policies, in the reactions it produces from other states, and in the responses to these reactions from others. In initiating one's own policies, irrationality can avoid large losses-of-face and policy disasters (stick-in-the-mud) or dramatically increase the range of policy options available (daredevil). In the reactions produced in others, irrationality can minimize negative reactions through external predictability (stick-in-the-mud) or through resisting the logic of submission (daredevil). In one's responses to these reactions, irrationality can help to create an image of refusal-to-budge (stick-in-the-mud) or of credible automatic responses (daredevil).

Without doubt dangers exist in the application of irrationality even under the most advantageous circumstances. Stick-in-the-mud irrationality could lead to an inappropriate rigidity and premature exclusion of innovation and result in a cumulatively irreversible policy quagmire. Daredevil irrationality could lead to a total loss of credibility and heightened international resentment. But it may be possible to control these dangers to some extent through selective use of irrationality—Schelling,[19] for example, points out that states can manipulate their own rationality beneficially by suspending it for a period of time and later regaining it. Indeed, an unpredictable "flip-flopping" between rationality and irrationality may be a desirable image or strategy for a nation to have.[20]

CASE FINDINGS ON THE UTILITY OF IRRATIONALITY

Not all of the contentions found in the literature receive supporting or opposing evidence from the twelve reviewed case studies, and some of the case patterns go well beyond these existing propositions. Table 2 summarizes the general pattern of results from the case studies with regard to stick-in-the-mud/daredevil fluctuation and the four dimensions of irrationality.

The insights described in the syntheses at the end of the four case study chapters help to explain when stick-in-the-mud and daredevil irrationality are most and least preferable in international confrontations. Stick-in-the-mud irrationality seems most likely to succeed when used in a deterrent, status quo fashion to maintain one's sphere of influence; and most likely to fail when used in a coercive, compellent, non–status quo fashion, particularly if the initiator has previously failed to forestall the current status quo and/or has vague, fluctuating goals in the confrontation. Daredevil irrationality seems most likely to succeed when the action occurs within one's sphere of influence, at least partially to protect one's own citizens, and can be quickly consolidated while surprise and a local power advantage persist; and most likely to fail when a repressive regime attempts to improve its internal/external image and needs a long-term power advantage to hold onto its gain.

The twelve reviewed cases also reveal some explanations of the patterns of effectiveness of the four dimensions of irrationality. Irrationality reflecting incompatibility of decisions with goals, consensus, or outcomes seems most likely to succeed when the initiator's actions do not require much intragovernmental coordination and/or when the initiator's government does not have a functioning checks-and-balances system; and most likely to fail when the ini-

Table 2
Summary of Case Study Patterns

Irrationality	Success	Failure
Stick-in-the-Mud	China-Kampuchea South Africa- Namibia USSR-Poland	US-Gas Pipeline US-Nicaragua Somalia-Ethiopia

Daredevil	Iran-US Hostages
	USSR-
	  Korean Airlines
	US-Grenada
		Iraq-Iran
		Argentina-
		  Falklands
		Libya-
		  Embassy Shooting

Incompatibility with
Goals, Consensus, or
Outcomes
	USSR-Poland
	USSR-
	  Korean Airlines
		US-Gas Pipeline
		US-Nicaragua
		Argentina-
		  Falklands

Non-Comprehensive
Search-and-
Evaluation
	South Africa-
	  Namibia
	USSR-Poland
	Iran-US Hostages
	USSR-
	  Korean Airlines
	US-Grenada
		US-Gas Pipeline
		US-Nicaragua
		Iraq-Iran
		Argentina-
		  Falklands

Inconsistency of
Statements and/or
Actions
	South Africa-
	  Namibia
	USSR-Poland
	USSR-
	  Korean Airlines
	US-Grenada
		US-Gas Pipeline
		US-Nicaragua
		Somalia-Ethiopia
		Iraq-Iran
		Libya-
		  Embassy Shooting

Non-Dispassionate
Style of Decision
	China-Kampuchea
	Iran-US Hostages
		US-Nicaragua
		Argentina-
		  Falklands
		Libya-
		  Embassy Shooting

tiator's intragovernmental coordination of actions seems critically important to cope with the challenge in a confrontation and/or to communicate resolve. In the Poland and Korean Airlines confrontations, the nature of Soviet action—subtle and indirect in the first case and quick and violent in the second—was such that subordinating Soviet national interests to petty bureaucratic motives in Poland and subordinating the overall Soviet political consensus to the desires of the Soviet military in downing the Korean jet did not significantly inhibit effectiveness. However, in the confrontations over the Soviet natural gas pipeline, Nicaragua, and the Falkland Islands, the incompatibilities with American elite consensus in the first two cases and with Argentine national interests in the third case undercut both the effectiveness of the actions taken and the resolve communicated because of the high coordination requirements of the multifaceted policies involved.

Irrationality reflecting non-comprehensive search-and-evaluation seems most likely to succeed when the target nation's behavior is relatively static throughout the confrontation due to the short decision time available or to the unavailability of alternative responses; and most likely to fail if the target develops unexpected adverse reactions to the initiator's move, requiring massive adjustments in policy. South Africa, the Soviet Union, Iran, and the United States faced relatively stable targets in the Namibia, Poland, Korean Airlines, American hostages, and Grenada confrontations; while the United States, Iraq, and Argentina faced active and belligerent targets full of creative countermeasures in the Soviet gas pipeline, Nicaragua, Iran, and Falkland Islands confrontations. When the target's counter-actions are non-existent or relatively unchanging, there is no reason for the initiator to perform a systematic evaluation of its own or its adversary's behavior, and such an evaluation could even result in an image of weakness or lack of policy perseverance.

Irrationality reflecting inconsistency of statements and/or actions seems most likely to succeed when used to conceal and cloud the initiator's brutal direct application of superior power; and most likely to fail when the target interprets this inconsistency as weakness, lack of commitment, or confusion about goals or strategies. South Africa, the Soviet Union, and the United States all have employed inconsistency successfully to mitigate the negative reactions to their applications of overwhelming power against Namibia, Poland, Korea, and Grenada. But when the United States, Somalia, Iraq, and Libya exhibited inconsistency in the Soviet gas pipeline, Nicaragua, Ethiopia, Iran, and Britain confrontations, the target state in each case associated the inconsistency with the initiator's lack of resolve. Failure resulted in this second set of cases because the targets viewed the initiators' inconsistency as so severe or significant that it obscured the initiators' credibility and sense of mission.

Finally, irrationality reflecting non-dispassionate style of decision seems most likely to succeed when the initiating government's focus is to fan the flames of anger and resistance toward an enemy in order to prevent the adversary from gaining or consolidating control in the confrontation; and most likely to fail when the initiating government's focus is suppressing resistance to itself and its policies so as to consolidate its own control in the confrontation. China and Iran both were effective in displaying emotionalism toward Vietnam and the United States to reduce these adversaries' influence in the area of confrontation; while the United States, Argentina, and Libya all were ineffective in their emotional outbursts toward Nicaragua and Britain designed to increase their own influence and control. It thus appears that emotionalism is more successful in creating hatred, antagonism, and opposition toward another group than in directly fostering loyalty and support for oneself (or one's puppets) due to the immense psychological satisfaction derived from scapegoating.

COMPARING PREVAILING CONTENTIONS TO CASE FINDINGS

A careful juxtaposition of the largely deductively derived contentions about the utility of irrationality with the inductively derived patterns in the case studies reveals some crucial differences. With regard to stick-in-the-mud irrationality, the cases support the contention that it can beneficially increase the stability and predictability of policies, as in the case of South Africa in Namibia. But the cases do not support the contention that the stick-in-the-mud approach serves to avoid a large external loss-of-face or policy disaster because the stick-in-the-mud failures—the U.S.-pipeline, U.S.-Nicaragua, and Somalia-Ethiopia cases—involved outcomes just as humiliating or crippling to the initiator as do non-stick-in-the-mud situations. Furthermore, the cases undermine the contention that stick-in-the-mud irrationality does not generate hostile reactions from others due to its external predictability, as shown in the massive opposition engendered by the American threat to major interests in the gas pipeline and Nicaragua cases; and the contention that stick-in-the-mud irrationality generates a convincing image of resolve due to its consistency, as shown in the preclusion of such an image by Somalia's series of futile actions. However, the cases display the advantage of a deterrent, status quo application of stick-in-the-mud irrationality which is not identified in existing contentions.

For daredevil irrationality, the cases support the contention that it can increase the menu of policy options, particularly alternatives involving short-term surprise (as in the case of Iran seizing the American hostages), and the contention that daredevil irrationality can help in the creation of credible automatic responses (as in the case of Soviet response to violation of its airspace). But the cases do not support the claim that daredevil irrationality helps to preclude negative reactions due to its unpredictability and resistance to the logic of submission, as wars triggered by Iraq and Argentina demonstrate. However, the cases do indicate the benefits of applying daredevil irrationality when the confrontation at least indirectly involves protecting one's own citizens, and this assertion does not appear in the existing literature.

Turning to the four dimensions of irrationality, several disparities again emerge from this comparative analysis of prevailing propositions and case study patterns. Regarding incompatibility of decisions with goals, consensus, or outcomes, the cases most directly support—as exemplified by the Soviet Union in the Poland and Korean Airlines incidents—the contention that such incompatibility can lead to internal success more when the initiating state's motivations reflect internal political power factions than when they reflect the non-bureaucratic calculation of external policy effectiveness. The cases do not address many existing contentions, but the claim which the cases most directly oppose is that incompatibility is preferable if the government possesses little information on the confrontation: in the United States, for instance, the quality of information on Nicaragua among most policy-making groups has been low, but this deficiency has not caused the American policy's incompatibilities to produce a successful outcome. Deviating from an uninformed consensus need not yield effective policy. However, the cases do show the advantage of this incompatibility when the confrontation does not need much intragovernmental coordination, and the literature on irrationality does not directly address this point.

With respect to non-comprehensive search-and-evaluation used to support sluggish and stagnant policies, the cases most directly support the assertion, as evidenced by South Africa in Namibia, that this irrational process can function effectively if critical decision resources such as accurate information are lacking. But the cases oppose the contention that such a process is more successful when not preceded by a long and paralyzing series of incremental policies; the sluggishness of previous policies did not seem critical in explaining the outcomes of confrontations. Regarding non-comprehensive search-and-evaluation of a rash and reckless nature, the cases supported the contention that this irrational process can be preferable if facing a restrained and conciliatory state: the Carter Administration thus presented a perfect target for Khomeini, while Britain was a poor target for Argentina because the Thatcher Administration was neither restrained nor conciliatory. To these contentions the cases add that non-comprehensive search-and-evaluation is most likely to be successful if the target state's behavior is relatively static, an assertion not dealt with in the prevailing literature.

Turning to inconsistency of statements and/or actions, the cases provide support for the claim, as demonstrated in the Korean Airlines and Grenada cases, that such inconsistency can be effective when used infrequently and in the short-term to avoid low credibility and high distrust. While the cases do not address some existing assertions, a couple of them are directly challenged: if a nation has a clear image of vulnerability, inconsistency may not help out because—as in the case of Somalia—the inconsistency may simply communicate refusal to recognize the reality of a dire situation; and if a confrontation involves rapidly changing circumstances, inconsistency again may not be preferable because—as in the cases of the United States in Nicaragua and Iraq in Iran—the inconsistency may simply communicate an inability to cope effectively with change. However, the cases do reveal a pattern not found among prevailing contentions—that inconsistency of statements and/or actions is likely to be successful when used to cloud the initiator's brutal application of superior power.

Finally, in examining non-dispassionate style of decision, the case evidence, particularly the Iranian seizure of American hostages, supports the contention that such emotionalism can be preferable when a nation has a low reputation for resolve and credibility and wants to communicate strong intent. There was a conspicuous absence of caring emotions playing on international sympathy in the confrontations, for as one would expect hostility and vindictiveness played the central role, and so the claims about the utility of caring emotions cannot be evaluated. However, there is a pattern of success in the cases when the initiating government uses emotionalism to foster anger and resistance toward an enemy in order to prevent it from gaining or consolidating control in a confrontation, and this pattern does not explicitly emerge in the literature's claims.

Aside from these findings specific to particular facets of irrationality, some more general trends which appeared in the twelve case studies have only an indirect relationship with prevailing wisdom on the subject. All of the successful displays of irrationality, with the exception of that in the Iran hostage crisis, involved initiators with massive overall power advantages over the targets, reinforcing the common belief that irrationality used by national governments cannot seriously expect to overturn the international power pecking order. Nonetheless, possessing a significant power advantage is clearly not sufficient for the effectiveness of irrationality, as the American failure in Nicaragua graphically illustrates. Most of the initiators of the irrational moves in the confrontations, with the exceptions of China in Kampuchea and Iraq in Iran, became victims of relative diplomatic isolation as a result of these moves. The lack of impact this isolation had on the success of these moves shows how irrationality frequently circumvents traditional alliance and international law/opinion restraints. Throughout the cases, the critical nature of the actions' relationship to the initiators' spheres of influence indicates that irrationality has severe geographical constraints. None of the confrontations not initiated by a superpower escalated into a superpower confrontation, suggesting the relative containability of irrationality applications. The frequent entrance of wishful thinking into the initiating states' miscalculations shows that, at least in confrontations involving irrationality, the dominance of optimistic desires over pessimistic expectations is not uncommon among foreign policy makers. Last, none of these confrontations had their outcomes directly influenced by the presence of nuclear weapons in the initiating states, and none moved closer to the actual use of nuclear weapons due to the tensions involved in the confrontation.

8.

Policy Implications

The patterns in the irrationality case studies naturally suggest some policy implications both in initiating and reacting to irrationality. While this study has attempted to avoid taking a value position regarding the moral/ethical reprehensibility of consciously manipulating irrationality for one's own gain, there is a need for prescription both to show those who value such use of irrationality how to exploit it for their own advantage, and to show those who find irrationality dangerous or loathsome how to protect themselves from it. This chapter outlines these alternative policy prescriptions, which are extremely tentative, and then concludes with a discussion of the global implications of proliferating irrationality.

Dror well expresses the complexity of attempting to generate policy advice in any direction concerning irrationality, which he calls "craziness":

> A first question is, How should a crazy state try to hide the features of its craziness? (A converse question is, How should a normal state try to present itself as crazy?) As long as a crazy state is expecting possible counteraction by other multiactors to its crazy features, before it is ready to absorb them, efforts to hide craziness are preferable. But, from a certain point, a crazy state may show off its craziness, and take advantage of the unwillingness of the other multiactors to make the investment needed to counter craziness. A subissue is, Should a somewhat crazy state try to make the impression of

a more extreme state of craziness, such as the crazy nonin-strumental state or a crazy martyr state? In particular, it may be shrewd to create the impression of a martyr crazy state since accommodation of this type of crazy state is often easier and cheaper than taking more extreme countermeasures.[1]

The case studies have reaffirmed that it is next to impossible to determine from available evidence when a country's irrationality is unintentional—the nation is truly "crazy"; when the irrationality is an intentional, premeditated, manipulated ruse to deceive the target and/or the rest of the world; and when a state's irrationality does not really exist and is simply the distorted and misguided product of misperceptions from the target and/or the rest of the world. The case studies have also demonstrated that it is relatively difficult to make across-the-board distinctions between rational and irrational states, for even the "reasonable" superpowers have ex-hibited on occasion rash irrationality; all one can do is to distinguish rational from irrational behavior by nations in particular situations. Given these two limitations (as well as Dror's earlier cautions), this chapter simply provides advice on how states who wish to apply or avoid irrationality may do so. While some nations cannot control the exact conditions under which they exhibit irrationality, even the most irrational states seem to have some level of discipline regarding the timing and targets of their irrational outbursts.

PRESCRIPTIONS FOR APPLYING IRRATIONALITY

For nations which see utility in irrationality to serve their national interests, or which are drawn for other reasons to the application of irrationality, it is perhaps obvious that one would advocate ir-rationality only if it were more cost-effective than the more tradi-tional means of attaining one's goals. If standard diplomatic approaches, straightforward military escapades, or economic sanc-tions seem less costly and risky and more beneficial as a means to a desired end, then these policies are preferable to irrationality.

One key consideration in the use of irrationality is the nature of the target state's decision-making or information-processing system in dealing with the confrontation. Although the cases did not comprehensively examine the targets in the confrontations, it appears that—with the glaring exception of the abortive Iraqi invasion of Iran—the target was generally at least as rational (and sometimes more so) than the initiator. There seems to be a real advantage to initiating irrationality against a rational target: stick-in-the-mud approaches wear down the resistance of a rational adversary, and daredevil approaches shock this opponent with unprepared-for moves.

Another feature essential to employing irrationality is the ability of the initiating state to pull off its exercise of irrationality in the particular confrontation. If the application of irrationality involves intentional deception—disguising of motives or methods—then only states with centralized control of information and effective internal and international propaganda should undertake such an approach. The greater success by the Soviet Union over the United States in irrationality displays at least potentially exemplifies this need. If the application of irrationality creates the probable alienation of the initiator's allies or supporters, then the initiator should be able to withstand withdrawal of this support. Iran in the hostage seizure and South Africa in the Namibia dispute were able to withstand this withdrawal; the United States in the gas pipeline controversy and Somalia in the Ethiopia conflict were not.

A third aspect of the decision to apply irrationality is the relationship between the initiator and the target with respect to the issue of the confrontation. The optimal situation for using irrationality seems to be when the target state recognizes the legitimate right of the intervening state to involve itself in the confrontation, as was the case for the Soviet Union in Poland and China in Kampuchea. The basis for this legitimacy relates to the historic relationship between the existing governments of the initiator and target and/or the past activity of the initiator in the area of confrontation. Irrationality seems least appropriate when there is no such target recognition of legitimate initiator involvement, as in the cases of the United States in Nicaragua and Libya in the London embassy shooting.

Beyond these general considerations, the preceding chapter's analysis of the utility and disutility of irrationality suggests more specific policy recommendations. States should use stick-in-the-mud irrationality when they need to enhance the stability and predictability of policies, particularly in pursuit of deterrent, status quo goals within one's sphere of influence. States should use daredevil irrationality when they need innovative policy alternatives involving short-term surprise or credible automatic responses, particularly if a confrontation involves protecting the initiating state's own citizens. States should use irrationality involving incompatibility with goals, consensus, or outcomes when self-interested internal political power factions have excessive dominance in the initiator's government or when a confrontation does not need much intragovernmental coordination. States should use irrationality reflecting non-comprehensive search-and-evaluation when it is impossible to attain adequate information during a confrontation and when the target state is restrained, conciliatory, and relatively static in its response to the initiator. States should use irrationality reflecting inconsistency of statements and/or actions when done infrequently and when done to cloud the initiator's application of superior power against the target. Finally, states should use irrationality involving non-dispassionate style when lacking reputation for resolve and wanting to communicate strong intent or when desiring to foster anger toward an enemy to prevent it from gaining or consolidating control in a confrontation.

PRESCRIPTIONS FOR RESISTING IRRATIONALITY

Although neither the theoretical propositions cited from existing literature nor the twelve case studies focus on when and how nations can respond effectively if confronted with irrational behavior by others, some admittedly more far-fetched policy implications do emerge from this study in this regard. These prescriptions seem particularly important because many government decision makers are more concerned with defending themselves against internal and external irrationality than in exhibiting irrationality themselves. Currently in the international arena there seems to be almost a paranoia among Western developed nations about how to forestall irrational behavior they find incomprehensible and unjustifiable, not a curiosity about how to use irrationality for their own purposes.

Dror[2] is one of the very few policy analysts who suggests specific methods of countering irrational states, and he asserts that "the most effective and efficient way to handle the possibility of crazy states is (1) to prevent the crazy state from happening; (2) if it happens, to prevent it from getting more crazy; and (3) to prevent it from achieving external-action capabilities." More specifically, for dealing with these irrational states he recommends reducing conditions encouraging craziness in them, reducing the flow of military knowledge and hardware to them; detecting early their emergence; avoiding giving in to them; encouraging alliances against them; deterring them through obvious actions they cannot ignore aimed at values they regard highly; destroying their external-action capability; stimulating revolt in them; occupying them; limiting the range of damage they can cause; and bargaining with them to win time.

In order for nations confronting irrationality to have a realistic chance of carrying out these policy options, Dror[3] contends they have to be willing (1) to take action against irrational states even before a visible threat emerges; (2) to pay a short-term price to avoid the longer-range threat; (3) to overcome the traditional concepts of the sovereignty and equality of all states, and (4) to develop novel types of actions. He points out with regret[4] that there is a very low probability that any of these preconditions will be met, and thus that any of his preferred strategies will be implemented, because government decision makers focus on immediate problems and reactive policies, prefer low-risk policies, display policy conservatism, operate under severe domestic political constraints, and face a loose bipolar system which increases the chances of an irrational state gaining support from one of the superpowers.

While Dror's policy advice contains some valuable insights (despite some morally questionable premises), it seems quite sweeping and overly pessimistic about both the feasibility of countering irrationality and the policy options available to do so. There appear to be three categories of policy recommendations for resisting irrationality: (1) perception manipulation and propaganda, (2) improvement in decision-making systems, and (3) clarification and escalation of punitive actions. This policy advice applies both to preventing the emergence of irrationality and to reducing it once it has emerged, and both to resisting irrationality from other governments and to resisting it within one's own government. Of course, given this book's central argument about the pervasiveness of irrationality, it would be impossible to stamp out irrational behavior using any method; so the suggestions which follow are more along the lines of counter-punches than knockout blows.

Examining first the counter-irrationality approach of perception manipulation and propaganda, a variety of strategies seem available. The broadest scheme would be to launch an internationally harmonized (involving more than one nation), two-pronged assault on irrationality attacking both its legitimacy and its effectiveness. Such an assault could portray irrationality as illegitimate because, when it is manipulated rather than genuine, it violates the prevailing ethical/moral/religious norms of honesty and straightforwardness; and, when it is genuine rather than manipulated, it is flagrantly and unjustifiedly underreactive or overreactive in the context of the range of coercive and non-coercive instruments of influence in international relations. This assault could emphasize the ineffectiveness of irrationality, especially for states immune to the illegitimacy arguments, by underscoring the likelihood of stick-in-the-mud decisions leading to rigid, cumulatively irreversible policy quagmires and of daredevil decisions leading to reduced credibility and dramatically increased global resentment. For countering the effectiveness specifically of manipulated irrationality, the focus could be on the high risk of discovery and backfire of the deception, given the increasingly sophisticated surveillance mechanisms promoting better detection of true intentions, capabilities, and actions.

The circumstances under which the reviewed confrontation cases failed suggest more detailed policy prescriptions for resisting irrationality through perception manipulation and propaganda. To counter stick-in-the-mud irrationality, one could portray the irrational state to the target state and the world as being coercive, compellent, and non–status quo with fluctuating goals; and to counter daredevil irrationality, one could convince the irrational state itself that it would need a long-term power advantage to hold on to any gain achieved. Strategies for countering each of irrationality's dimensions are as follows: for incompatibility with goals, consensus, or outcomes, foster governmental divisiveness if coordination is needed; for non-comprehensive search-and-evaluation, increase the target's confidence to make unexpected counter-moves; for inconsistency of statements and/or actions, convince the target that the initiator's inconsistency means weakness, lack of commit-ment, or confusion; and for non-dispassionate style, portray the initiator as motivated by a desire to consolidate its control. Needless to say, all of these options are more easily said than done.

Turning to the second category of counter-irrationality ap-proaches—improvement in decision-making systems—policy op-tions emerge which could be both implemented within one's own nation and actively fostered abroad. Change in the recruitment procedures for government decision makers appears to be a first step, with the goal being to attract and retain officials with improved capabilities in logic and reasoning, systematic and comprehensive analysis, and dispassionate judgments. Training and indoctrination of these officials could improve to reinforce these rational traits, to increase technical proficiency for dealing with particular issues, and to reduce common perceptual distortions. This training would need to include educating decision makers to accept the desirability of long-term, non-reactive measures resisting irrationality. Another strategy would be to alter government structures so as to insulate foreign policy makers from certain pressures, such as bureaucratic power plays, deemed as irrational from the viewpoint of maximizing the state's effectiveness and efficiency. There could be more em-phasis placed on improving the quality of relevant information available to decision makers, especially during crises, and on re-ducing the time pressure involved in key decisions. Clandestine intelligence collection could focus more on states (and individuals) exhibiting irrationality. Last, accountability for decisions could in-crease for both agencies and individual officials, promoting earlier detection and reduction of irrationality in the decision process.

The final category of counter-irrationality approaches, clarifica-tion and escalation of punitive actions, can also apply both inter-nally and externally. In resisting irrationality from other nations, these punitive measures would need to go well beyond the diplo-matic isolation so prevalent and so ineffective in the case studies. What is needed is internationally harmonized (more than one nation involved) economic and military sanctions automatically applied to the initiating irrational state and its supporters. While such an ap-proach would doubtlessly face all of the stumbling blocks of col-lective security and balance-of-power systems in the past, to work against irrationality it would need more cohesiveness and more

severe measures than any of these past systems. In resisting irrationality within one's own government, the solution seems more
straightforward—dismiss or demote any individual bureaucrat or
bureaucratic group displaying a significantly damaging pattern of
irrationality. While these measures may seem stern, more subtle
disincentives rarely appear to be effective in curtailing irrational
behavior.

In comparing these three categories of irrationality measures, and
taking into account both short-term and long-term feasibility
(which admittedly is low for the ideal forms of the measures) and
effectiveness, it appears that perception manipulation and propaganda would be the most desirable, improvement in decision-making systems the next most desirable, and clarification and escalation
of punitive measures the least desirable and only to be used in cases
of last resort. This ranking seems to contradict prevailing wisdom
on resisting irrationality, which often chooses punitive action as the
optimum strategy because "that's all those crazies understand." The
reasons for the ranking here are (1) since image concerns are frequently the motive behind the use of irrationality, image manipulation would seem to be the most effective counter-strategy; and
(2) perception manipulation and propaganda seem to have the low-
est risks and costs if they fail and/or escalate beyond initial
expectations.

GLOBAL CONSEQUENCES OF PROLIFERATING
IRRATIONALITY

It appears that a world composed largely or entirely of irrational
nations would have quite damaging international system consequences. For both stick-in-the-mud and daredevil variants, a critical
tradeoff seems to exist between benefits to one's own state and costs
to the system as a whole. A world full of stick-in-the-mud states
would be unlikely to progress or improve, would operate on the
basis of "worst-case" analysis, and would suffer extremely protracted conflicts. A world full of daredevil states would promote
international anarchy, paranoic and hostile perceptions, and violent
and costly conflict.

What these two dire hypothetical global scenarios demonstrate is that the utility of irrationality is mainly for the irrational state alone, when irrationality is used only intermittently over time and the rest of the world is composed largely of nations which think and act rationally most of the time. The real advantage of an irrational decision in world politics is to be able to benefit from the temporary absence of many of the rational constraints under which the rest of the world normally operates; in a sense, irrationality affords a chance to play the game of nations by a new set of rules, one that is not yet well understood or manipulated by most countries in the international system.

This book is directed more toward provocation than proof. This analysis has attempted to take a first step in showing when, how, and why irrationality can be more or less effective as a policy foundation in international confrontations. On the basis of juxtaposing theoretical assertions to the findings from the case studies, crucial conditions have emerged broadly explaining the success and failure of stick-in-the-mud and daredevil irrationality, and more specifically the results of incompatibility of decisions with goals, consensus, and outcomes, non-comprehensive search-and-evaluation, inconsistency of statements and/or actions, and non-dispassionate style of decision. These conditions served as the springboard for some preliminary policy prescriptions for using or resisting irrationality in international relations. One is drawn to the conclusion that nations not only frequently behave irrationally, but sometimes should not strive to become more rational.

There is a desperate need given today's rapidly changing and unpredictable international system for further scholarly investigation of this topic and for refinement of the findings presented here. The inveterate association of irrationality with stupidity in international relations needs to be drastically re-evaluated and challenged.

Notes

INTRODUCTION

1. Steven J. Brams, *Superpower Games: Applying Game Theory to Superpower Conflict* (New Haven: Yale University Press, 1985), xi.

2. Klaus Knorr, "Strategic Surprise: The Incentive Structure" in Klaus Knorr and Patrick Morgan, eds., *Strategic Military Surprise: Incentives and Opportunities* (New Brunswick, N.J.: Transaction Books, 1983), 192.

3. Donald R. Kinder and Janet A. Weiss, "In Lieu of Rationality: Psychological Perspectives on Foreign Policy Decision Making," *Journal of Conflict Resolution*, 22 (1978): 728.

4. Yehezkel Dror, *Crazy States* (Millwood, N.Y.: Kraus, 1980), xvii-xviii.

5. Nigel Howard, *Paradoxes of Rationality* (Cambridge: MIT Press, 1971), 6.

6. Dror, *Crazy States*, xv.

CHAPTER 1

1. Alexander L. George, *Presidential Decisionmaking in Foreign Policy: The Effective Use of Information and Advice* (Boulder, Colo.: Westview Press, 1980), 2.

2. James E. Dougherty and Robert L. Pfaltzgraff, *Contending Theories of International Relations* (Philadelphia: J.B. Lippincott, 1971), 266.

3. Janice Gross Stein and Raymond Tanter, *Rational Decision Making: Israel's Security Choices, 1967* (Columbus: Ohio State University Press, 1980), 10.

4. Nigel Howard, *Paradoxes of Rationality* (Cambridge: MIT Press, 1971), 6.

5. Herbert A. Simon, *Reason in Human Affairs* (Stanford: Stanford University Press, 1983), 37–38, 72.

6. John D. Steinbruner, *The Cybernetic Theory of Decision* (Princeton: Princeton University Press, 1974), chap. 2; and Glenn H. Snyder and Paul Diesing, *Conflict Among Nations* (Princeton: Princeton University Press, 1977), chap. 5.

7. George, *Presidential Decisionmaking*, 2.

8. Robert Jervis, *Perception and Misperception in International Politics* (Princeton: Princeton University Press, 1976), 119.

9. Stein and Tanter, *Rational Decision Making*, 13.

10. Herbert Simon, "A Behavioral Model of Rational Choice," *Journal of Economics*, 69 (1955): 99–118.

11. Charles E. Lindblom, "The Science of 'Muddling Through'," *Public Administration Review*, 19 (1959): 79–88.

12. Irving L. Janis, *Victims of Groupthink* (Boston: Houghton Mifflin, 1972).

13. Stanley Benn and G.W. Mortimore (eds.), *Rationality and the Social Sciences* (London: Routledge and Kegan Paul, 1976), 4.

14. Janice Gross Stein, "Can Decision Makers Be Rational and Should They Be? Evaluating the Quality of Decisions" in Michael Brecher, ed., *Studies in Crisis Behavior* (New Brunswick, N.J.: Transaction Books, 1978), 329.

15. Nelson Goodman, *Ways of World Making* (Indianapolis: Hackett, 1978), 124–25.

16. Simon, *Reason*, 5.

17. Ibid., 29–30.

18. Lloyd S. Etheredge, *A World of Men: The Private Sources of American Foreign Policy* (Cambridge: MIT Press, 1978), 46.

19. Irving L. Janis and Leon Mann, *Decision Making* (New York: Free Press, 1977), 45.

20. Patrick M. Morgan, *Deterrence: A Conceptual Analysis* (Beverly Hills, Calif.: Sage, 1977), 102.

21. Robert Mandel, "Psychological Approaches to International Relations" in Margaret G. Hermann, ed., *Political Psychology* (San Francisco: Jossey-Bass, 1986), 251–78.

22. Jack L. Snyder, "Rationality at the Brink: The Role of Cognitive Processes in Failures of Deterrence," *World Politics*, 30 (1978): 347; and Etheredge, *A World of Men*, chap. 2.

23. Stein, "Can Decision Makers Be Rational," 336.

24. Dougherty and Pfaltzgraff, *Contending Theories*, 316–17.

25. Graham T. Allison, *Essence of Decision* (Boston: Little, Brown, 1971), chaps. 3 and 4.

26. Robert Axelrod (ed.), *Structure of Decision* (Princeton: Princeton University Press, 1976), 241.

27. Joseph Frankel, *The Making of Foreign Policy: An Analysis of Decision Making* (London: Oxford University Press, 1963), 168–69.

28. Robert Mandel, *Perception, Decision Making, and Conflict* (Washington, D.C.: University Press of America, 1979), chap. 7.

29. Dean G. Pruitt, "Definition of the Situation as a Determinant of International Action" in Herbert C. Kelman, ed., *International Behavior* (New York: Holt, Rinehart, and Winston, 1965), 391–432.

30. Janis and Mann, *Decision Making*, 59.

31. George, *Presidential Decisionmaking*, 38–39.

32. Frankel, *The Making of Foreign Policy*, 170.

33. Ralph K. White, *Nobody Wanted War: Misperception in Vietnam and Other Wars* (New York: Doubleday, 1970), chap. 8.

34. Sidney Verba, "Assumptions of Rationality and Non-Rationality in Models of the International System" in James N. Rosenau, ed., *International Politics and Foreign Policy* (revised edition) (New York: Free Press, 1969), 220.

35. Margaret G. Hermann, "Explaining Foreign Policy Behavior: Using Personality Characteristics of Political Leaders," *International Studies Quarterly*, 24 (1980), 7–46.

36. Bruce M. Russett and Harvey Starr, *World Politics: The Menu for Choice* (San Francisco: W.H. Freeman, 1981), 316–20; Stein, "Can Decision Makers Be Rational," 318; and Morgan, *Deterrence*, 102.

37. Hermann, "Explaining Foreign Policy," 13–14; and Verba, "Assumptions of Rationality," 221.

38. Simon, *Reason*, 23–28.

39. Jervis, *Perception and Misperception*, chap. 4; Mandel, *Perception*, chaps. 3 and 4; and Robert A. LeVine and Donald T. Campbell, *Ethnocentrism* (New York: John Wiley, 1972), 212–23.

40. Verba, "Assumptions of Rationality," 222.

41. Janis and Mann, *Decision Making*, 93.

42. Frankel, *The Making of Foreign Policy*, 169.

43. Ibid., 170.

44. Margaret G. Hermann, "Who Becomes a Political Leader? Some Societal and Regime Influences on Selection of a Head of State" in Lawrence S. Falkowski, ed., *Psychological Models in International Politics* (Boulder, Colo.: Westview Press, 1979), 39.

45. Verba, "Assumptions of Rationality," 221; Frankel, *The Making of Foreign Policy*, 172; and Morgan, *Deterrence*, 103.

46. Klaus Knorr, "Strategic Surprise: The Incentive Structure" in Klaus Knorr and Patrick Morgan, eds., *Strategic Military Surprise: Incentives and Opportunities* (New Brunswick, N.J.: Transaction Books, 1983), 191–92.

47. George, *Presidential Decisionmaking*, 35–36.

48. L.J. Savage, "The Theory of Statistical Decision," *Journal of the American Statistical Association* 46 (1951): 55–67.

49. Steinbruner, *The Cybernetic Theory*, 62.

50. Anthony Downs, *Inside Bureaucracy* (Boston: Little, Brown, 1967), 272–73.

51. Ole R. Holsti, *Crisis Escalation War* (Montreal: McGill-Queens University Press, 1972), chap. 5.

52. Richard C. Snyder, *Deterrence, Weapons, and Decision Making* (China Lake, Calif.: U.S. Naval Ordnance Test Station, 1961), 141.

53. J. Weldon Moffitt and Ross Stagner, "Perceptual Rigidity and Closure as a Function of Anxiety," *Journal of Abnormal and Social Psychology*, 52 (1956): 354–57.

54. Pruitt, "Definition of the Situation," 391–432.

55. Morgan, *Deterrence*, 198.

56. Pruitt, "Definition of the Situation," 395; Mandel, *Perception*, 54; and George, *Presidential Decisionmaking*, 48–49.

57. Stein, "Can Decision Makers Be Rational," 335; and Etheredge, *A World of Men*, 104.

58. Edward E. Jones and Richard E. Nisbett, "The Actor and the Observer: Divergent Perceptions of the Causes of Behavior" in Edward E. Jones and others, eds., *Attribution: Perceiving the Causes of Behavior* (Morristown, N.J.: General Learning Press, 1972), 93–94.

59. Janis, *Victims of Groupthink*, 198; and Morgan, *Deterrence*, 113.

60. Frankel, *The Making of Foreign Policy*, 168–69.

61. Robert Mandel and Sarah Clarke, "Intractability in International Bargaining" (Paper presented at the annual meeting of the International Studies Association, Philadelphia, 1981), 11–12.

62. Etheredge, *A World of Men*, 104.

63. Howard, *Paradoxes of Rationality*, 184.

64. Simon, *Reason*, 7–8.

65. Eugene J. Meehan, "Review of *Reason in Human Affairs*," *American Political Science Review*, 78 (1984): 889–90.

66. Jervis, *Perception and Misperception*, 119.

67. Simon, *Reason*, 3, 37–38.

CHAPTER 2

1. Alexander L. George and Richard Smoke, *Deterrence in American Foreign Policy: Theory and Practice* (New York: Columbia University Press, 1974), 95–97.

CHAPTER 3

1. Kishore Mahbubani, "The Kampuchean Problem: A Southeast Asian Perception," *Foreign Affairs* 62 (1983/84):413.

2. Paul D. Wolfowitz, "Cambodia: The Search for Peace" (Washington, D.C.: U.S. State Department Bureau of Public Affairs, September 11, 1984), 1.

3. Ibid.

4. Ibid.

5. Ibid.

6. Michael Leifer, "The Balance of Advantage in Indochina," *World Today*, 38 (1982): 232.

7. Justus M. van der Kroef, "Kampuchea: Diplomatic Gambits and Political Realities," *Orbis*, 28 (1984): 145; and Elizabeth Becker, "Kampuchea in 1983: Further from Peace," *Asian Survey*, 24 (1984): 39, 42.

8. Wolfowitz, "Cambodia," 1–2.

9. Van der Kroef, "Kampuchea," 150.

10. Ibid., 146.

11. Wolfowitz, "Cambodia," 2.

12. Becker, "Kampuchea," 41; and Van der Kroef, "Kampuchea," 148.

13. Van der Kroef, "Kampuchea," 148.

14. Wolfowitz, "Cambodia," 2.

15. Pao-Min Chang, "Some Reflections on the Sino-Vietnamese Conflict over Kampuchea," *International Affairs*, 59 (1983): 381.

16. Ibid., 385.

17. Ibid., 384.

18. Guo Yan and Dong Nan, "The Kampuchean Issue: Its Origins and Major Aspects," *Beijing Review*, 26 (1983): 18.

19. Van der Kroef, "Kampuchea," 151.

20. Chang, "Some Reflections," 381.

21. Mahbubani, "The Kampuchean Problem," 414.

22. Chang, "Some Reflections," 387–88.

23. Van der Kroef, "Kampuchea," 162.

24. Ibid., 146.

25. Mahbubani, "The Kampuchean Problem," 411.

26. Chang, "Some Reflections," 387.

27. Ibid., 382, 385–86, 388.

28. Pao-Min Chang, "Kampuchea in Chinese and Vietnamese Policies: The Root of the Conflict," *Studies in Comparative Communism*, 16 (1983): 220–21.

29. Yan and Nan, "The Kampuchean Issue," 19.

30. Mahbubani, "The Kampuchean Problem," 407.

31. "Guerrilla Warriors: Now the Kremlin Feels the Heat," *U.S. News and World Report*, 95 (August 8, 1983): 24.

32. Van der Kroef, "Kampuchea," 146, 152.

33. Robert Kaylor, "Hanoi Cements Its Grip on Kampuchea," *U.S. News and World Report*, 98 (April 1, 1985): 38–39.

34. Mahbubani, "The Kampuchean Problem," 417–18.

35. George W. Shepherd, Jr., "Breaking the Namibia Impasse," *Africa Today*, 29 (1982): 23.

36. Kenneth Grundy, "Namibia in International Politics," *Current History*, 81 (1982): 101–5.

37. "South Africa and Namibia," *Center Magazine*, 16 (1983): 42.

38. Shepherd, "Breaking the Namibia Impasse," 25.

39. Grundy, "Namibia," 101–5.

40. Ibid.

41. John Seiler, "South Africa and Namibia: Persistence, Misperception, and Ultimate Failure," *Journal of Modern African Studies*, 20 (1982): 711; and Grundy, "Namibia," 101–5.

42. Shepherd, "Breaking the Namibia Impasse," 26.

43. "For Our Next Trick," *Economist*, 288 (July 23, 1983): 32.

44. "South Africa and Namibia," 55; Grundy, "Namibia," 101–5; and Seiler, "South Africa," 709.

45. Seiler, "South Africa," 712.

46. Shepherd, "Breaking the Namibia Impasse," 29.

47. Seiler, "South Africa," 708.

48. "For Our Next Trick," 32.

49. "South Africa and Namibia," 53.

50. Grundy, "Namibia," 101–5.

51. "South Africa and Namibia," 48.

52. Ibid., 50.

53. Seiler, "South Africa," 698.

54. Ibid., 689.

55. Ibid., 690.

56. Shepherd, "Breaking the Namibia Impasse," 23.

57. Seiler, "South Africa," 699.

58. "For Our Next Trick," 32.

59. Ibid.

60. "South Africa and Namibia," 49.

61. Grundy, "Namibia," 101–5.

62. "South Africa and Namibia," 50.

63. F. Stephen Larrabbee, "Poland: The Permanent Crisis," *Orbis*, 25 (1981): 235.

64. Seweryn Bialer, "Poland and the Soviet Imperium," *Foreign Affairs*, 59 (1981): 524.

65. Larrabbee, "Poland," 235–36.

66. Adam Bromke, "Poland: The Cliff's Edge," *Foreign Policy*, no. 41 (1980/81): 155.

67. Bialer, "Poland," 530.

68. Foreign Policy Association, "Poland and the U.S.S.R.: Troubles in Workers' Paradise" in Chau T. Phan, ed., *World Politics 82/83* (Guilford, Conn.: Dushkin, 1982), 170–76.

69. Larrabbee, "Poland," 242.

70. Ibid., 233.

71. Foreign Policy Association, "Poland," 170–76.

72. Larrabbee, "Poland," 244.

73. William G. Hyland, "U.S.-Soviet Relations: The Long Road Back," *Foreign Affairs*, 60 (1982): 545.

74. "Soviets Loosen Their Grip on Eastern Europe," *U.S. News and World Report*, 95 (December 5, 1983): 38.

75. Walter Laqueur, "U.S.-Soviet Relations," *Foreign Affairs*, 62 (1984): 573.

76. Richard D. Anderson, Jr., "Soviet Decision-Making and Poland," *Problems of Communism*, 31 (1982): 22.

77. Ibid., 31.

78. Ibid., 22.

79. Ibid., 24.

80. Ibid., 35.

81. Ibid.

82. Ibid., 22.

83. Laqueur, "U.S.-Soviet Relations," 573.

CHAPTER 4

1. "Siberian Gas Pipeline and U.S. Export Controls," *Gist* (Washington, D.C.: U.S. Department of State Bureau of Public Affairs, October 1982), 1.

2. Miles Costick, "That Soviet Gas Pipeline to the West," *National Review*, 33 (1981): 956.

3. Ibid.

4. Jonathan P. Stern, "Specters and Pipe Dreams," *Foreign Policy*, no. 48 (1982): 28.

5. "Siberian Gas Pipeline," 1.

6. Stern, "Specters," 23–25.

7. Josef Joffe, "Europe and America: The Politics of Resentment (Cont'd)," *Foreign Affairs*, 61 (1983): 570.

8. Stern, "Specters," 29–30.

9. "Siberian Gas Pipeline," 2.

10. Ibid.

11. Stern, "Specters," 33.

12. Joffe, "Europe," 574.

13. Ibid., 571.

14. Stern, "Specters," 21.

15. Norman Crossland, "Transatlantic Tensions: Pipeline Diplomacy" in Chau T. Phan, ed., *World Politics 82/83* (Guilford, Conn.: Dushkin, 1982), 166.

16. Stern, "Specters," 35.

17. "The Pied Pipeline," *The New Republic*, 185 (December 16, 1981): 7–8.

18. Joffe, "Europe," 571.

19. Stern, "Specters," 33.

20. Ibid., 31.

21. Ibid., 34.

22. Joffe, "Europe," 576.

23. Stern, "Specters," 32.

24. Joffe, "Europe," 575.

25. Stern, "Specters," 35–36.

26. Joffe, "Europe," 575.

27. Piero Gleijeses, "Resist Romanticism," *Foreign Policy*, no. 54 (1984): 124.

28. Arturo J. Cruz, "Nicaragua's Imperiled Revolution," *Foreign Affairs*, 61 (1983): 1033.

29. Gleijeses, "Resist Romanticism," 134.

30. Richard H. Ullman, "At War with Nicaragua," *Foreign Affairs*, 62 (1983): 48.

31. Christopher Dickey, "Central America: From Quagmire to Cauldron," *Foreign Affairs*, 62 (1984): 686.

32. Cruz, "Nicaragua's Imperiled Revolution," 1042.

33. Gleijeses, "Resist Romanticism," 129–30.

34. Richard Fagen, "The Nicaragua Crisis," *Monthly Review*, 34 (1982): 2–3.

35. Ullman, "At War," 42.

36. Dickey, "Central America," 669.

37. Fagen, "The Nicaragua Crisis," 15.

38. Ibid., 1.

39. Ullman, "At War," 43.

40. Dickey, "Central America," 667.

41. Ullman, "At War," 40.

42. Ibid., 39.

43. Dickey, "Central America," 665–66.

44. Cruz, "Nicaragua's Imperiled Revolution," 1046.

45. Dickey, "Central America," 668.

46. Gleijeses, "Resist Romanticism," 136–37.

47. Ullman, "At War," 43.

48. Ibid., 55.

49. Gleijeses, "Resist Romanticism," 136.

50. Fagen, "The Nicaragua Crisis," 15.

51. Ullman, "At War," 54.

52. Fagen, "The Nicaragua Crisis," 15.

53. Ullman, "At War," 48.

54. Fagen, "The Nicaragua Crisis," 2.

55. Ullman, "At War," 52.

56. Ibid., 42.

57. Ibid., 56.

58. Ibid.

59. Gleijeses, "Resist Romanticism," 137.

60. Ullman, "At War," 41.

61. Ibid., 49.

62. William D. Rogers, "The United States and Latin America," *Foreign Affairs*, 63 (1985): 560, 563.

63. Ullman, "At War," 49–50.

64. James Mayall, "The National Question in the Horn of Africa," *World Today*, 39 (1983): 337.

65. Guy Arnold, "America's Ally in the Horn of Africa," *Africa Report*, 28 (1983): 52.

66. Mayall, "The National Question," 336.

67. Ibid., 339.

68. "Western War, Northern Danger," *Economist*, 285 (November 13, 1982): 44.

69. Mayall, "The National Question," 339.

70. "The Spectre of War," *Africa*, no. 132 (August 1982): 12; and "Western War," 44.

71. "Western War," 44.

72. "An Elusive Peace," *Africa*, no. 132 (August 1982): 17; and Arnold, "America's Ally," 51–52.

73. Mayall, "The National Question," 336.

74. Arnold, "America's Ally," 52.

75. Ibid.

76. Ibid., 53.

77. Ibid.

78. Mayall, "The National Question," 341.

79. Arnold, "America's Ally," 52.

80. Andrew Young, "The United States and Africa: Victory for Diplomacy," *Foreign Affairs*, 59 (1981): 665.

81. Arnold, "America's Ally," 52–53.

82. Ibid., 51.

83. Ibid., 52.

84. Ibid., 51–52.

85. Ibid., 53.

86. "An Elusive Peace," 16.

87. Arnold, "America's Ally," 51.

88. Ibid.

89. Mayall, "The National Question," 337.

90. Ibid., 340.

91. "The Spectre of War," 13.

92. Mayall, "The National Question," 336.

93. "Western War," 44.

94. Ibid.; Arnold, "America's Ally," 51.

95. Arnold, "America's Ally," 53.

96. "Between Two Foes," *Economist*, 286 (February 19, 1983): 58.

97. Mayall, "The National Question," 336, 339; "An Elusive Peace," 18.

98. "Between Two Foes," 58; "The Spectre of War," 13.

99. Arnold, "America's Ally," 52.

100. "Between Two Foes," 58.

CHAPTER 5

1. Roy Parvis Mottahedeh, "Iran's Foreign Devils," *Foreign Policy*, no. 38 (1980): 25–26.

2. "Test of U.S. Resolve," *U.S. News and World Report*, 87 (November 26, 1979): 32.

3. Eric Rouleau, "Khomeini's Iran," *Foreign Affairs*, 59 (1980): 11.

4. J.C. Hurewitz, "The Middle East: A Year of Turmoil," *Foreign Affairs*, 59 (1981): 546–47.

5. Ibid., 548–49.

6. Mottahedeh, "Iran's Foreign Devils," 19.

7. Ibid., 33.

8. Rouleau, "Khomeini's Iran," 11.

9. Ibid., 13.

10. "Iran: The Test of Wills," *Time*, 114 (November 26, 1979): 21.

11. "Test of U.S. Resolve," 32.

12. Angus Deming and Chris J. Harper, "Iran's Martyr Complex," *Newsweek*, 94 (November 26, 1979): 40.

13. "Iran," 21.

14. Mottahedeh, "Iran's Foreign Devils," 30.

15. Dennis Mullin, "A Regime of Fanatics—and a Dim Future," *U.S. News and World Report*, 87 (November 26, 1979): 33.

16. Mottahedeh, "Iran's Foreign Devils," 30–31.

17. "Iran," 21.

18. Hurewitz, "The Middle East," 547.

19. Rouleau, "Khomeini's Iran," 7; Mullin, "A Regime of Fanatics," 33.

20. Rouleau, "Khomeini's Iran," 16.

21. George J. Church, "Honorable Deal—or Ransom?," *Time*, 117 (February 2, 1981): 40.

22. Ibid.

23. Hurewitz, "The Middle East," 550.

24. Murray Sayle, "The Sakhalin Crisis: Charge and Counter-charge," *Far Eastern Economic Review*, 121 (September 22, 1983): 27.

25. Robert Manning, "Who Gave the Order?," *Far Eastern Economic Review*, 121 (September 15, 1983): 14.

26. Tim Ahern, "Mystery Still Surrounds Flight 007 Tragedy," *Sunday Oregonian* (August 26, 1984): A2; and Ed Magnuson, "Fallout from Flight 007," *Time*, 124 (September 10, 1984): 16.

27. Sayle, "The Sakhalin Crisis," 28; Magnuson, "Fallout," 16.

28. Magnuson, "Fallout," 16.

29. William Lowther and David Cox, "The Mysteries of KAL Flight 007," *Maclean's*, 97 (April 9, 1984): 8; and Magnuson, "Fallout," 16.

30. Magnuson, "Fallout," 16.

31. Lowther and Cox, "The Mysteries," 8.

32. Seymour M. Hersh, *"The Target Is Destroyed"* (New York: Random House, 1986), chap. 14.

33. Ahern, "Mystery," A2.

34. Ibid.

35. Lowther and Cox, "The Mysteries," 9; Magnuson, "Fallout," 16.

36. Hersh, *"The Target is Destroyed"*, chap. 17.

37. Manning, "Who Gave the Order?," 14.

38. Ibid.

39. Ahern, "Mystery," A2.

40. Magnuson, "Fallout," 16.

41. "Russia's Robber Barons," *Far Eastern Economic Review*, 121 (September 22, 1983): 30.

42. Joseph Fromm, "Trigger-Happy Soviets—A Jolt to Relations with U.S.," *U.S. News and World Report*, 95 (September 12, 1983): 24.

43. Nick Ludington, "Soviet Image, Power Survive; U.S. Reaction Proves Costly," *Sunday Oregonian* (August 26, 1984): A2.

44. "Transcript of Soviet Official's Statement and Excerpts from News Session" in Suzanne P. Ogden, ed., *World Politics 84/85* (Guilford, Conn.: Dushkin, 1984), 70–74.

45. "Airborne Aggression: A Soviet Trademark," *U.S. News and World Report*, 95 (September 12, 1983): 25.

46. Ahern, "Mystery," A2.

47. Hersh, *"The Target Is Destroyed,"* 249.

48. "Time Is Running Out," *New Statesman*, 106 (September 9, 1983): 3.

49. Sayle, "The Sakhalin Crisis," 28, 30.

50. Peter Calvocoressi, "How Russia Hit an 'Own Goal'," *Sunday Times* (September 11, 1983): 16.

51. Ibid.

52. Hersh, *"The Target Is Destroyed,"* 221.

53. "Russia's Robber Barons," 30.

54. "Time Is Running Out," 3.

55. "Russia's Robber Barons," 30.

56. Lowther and Cox, "The Mysteries," 8.

57. Ibid., 12.

58. Ibid.

59. Magnuson, "Fallout," 16.

60. Lowther and Cox, "The Mysteries," 8.

61. Ibid., 12.

62. Ludington, "Soviet Image," A2.

63. Tony Thorndike, "The Grenada Crisis," *World Today*, 39 (1983): 470.

64. United States Department of State and Department of Defense, *Grenada: A Preliminary Report* (Washington, D.C.: U S. Government Printing Office, December 16, 1983), 8.

65. Thorndike, "The Grenada Crisis," 473.

66. United States Department of State and Department of Defense, *Grenada*, 33–34.

67. Thorndike, "The Grenada Crisis," 468.

68. Ibid., 469.

69. United States Department of State and Department of Defense, *Grenada*, 2.

70. Ibid.

71. "Anatomy of a Little War," *The New Republic*, 189 (November 21, 1983): 7.

72. Christopher Dickey, "Central America: From Quagmire to Caul-

dron," *Foreign Affairs*, 62 (1984): 691; and United States Department of State and Department of Defense, *Grenada*, 2.

73. "Anatomy," 8.

74. Thorndike, "The Grenada Crisis," 475.

75. Ibid., 468.

76. "Anatomy," 8–9.

77. Ibid., 7.

78. Thorndike, "The Grenada Crisis," 468; Dickey, "Central America," 691.

79. "Anatomy," 9.

80. Dickey, "Central America," 691.

81. United States Department of State and Department of Defense, *Grenada*, 41.

82. Thorndike, "The Grenada Crisis," 468.

83. "Anatomy," 9.

84. Dickey, "Central America," 690.

85. Ibid., 691.

86. Thorndike, "The Grenada Crisis," 475.

87. Ibid., 470; Dickey, "Central America," 689.

88. Dickey, "Central America," 691; Thorndike, "The Grenada Crisis," 470.

89. Thorndike, "The Grenada Crisis," 470.

90. Ibid., 475.

91. Dickey, "Central America," 691–92.

92. Ibid., 692.

93. United States Department of State and Department of Defense, *Grenada*, i.

94. Susanna McBee, "They Still Love the Yanks in Grenada, But—," *U.S. News and World Report*, 97 (August 6, 1984): 27.

95. Thorndike, "The Grenada Crisis," 476.

CHAPTER 6

1. Tareq Y. Ismael, *Iraq and Iran: Roots of Conflict* (Syracuse, N.Y.: Syracuse University Press, 1982), 1–2.

2. Ibid., 22.

3. Claudia Wright, "Implications of the Iraq-Iran War," *Foreign Affairs*, 59 (1980/81): 278.

4. Harvey Sicherman, "Iraq and Iran at War: The Search for Security," *Orbis*, 24 (1981): 712.

5. Ismael, *Iraq and Iran*, 27.

6. Wright, "Implications," 279.

7. Ibid., 280.

8. Richard Cottam, "The Iran-Iraq War," *Current History*, 83 (1984): 11.

9. "Iran-Iraq War," *Gist* (Washington, D.C.: U.S. Department of State Bureau of Public Affairs, November 1983), 1.

10. Michael Sterner, "The Iran-Iraq War," *Foreign Affairs*, 63 (1984): 129.

11. "Iran-Iraq War," *Gist* (Washington, D.C.: U.S. Department of State Bureau of Public Affairs, May 1985), 1; and Dilip Hiro and Michael Dobbs, "Two Warring Capitals," *Washington Post* (October 23, 1986): A25.

12. Cottam, "The Iran-Iraq War," 9.

13. William Drozdiak, "Iran-Iraq War Takes on Life of Its Own," *Providence Sunday Journal* (March 11, 1984): A–6.

14. "Iran-Iraq War" (1983), 1–2.

15. Cottam, "The Iran-Iraq War," 11.

16. Sterner, "The Iran-Iraq War," 129.

17. Cottam, "The Iran-Iraq War," 11–12.

18. Joseph J. Sisco, "Middle East: Progress or Lost Opportunity?," *Foreign Affairs*, 61 (1983): 615; and Drozdiak, "Iran-Iraq War," A–6.

19. Sterner, "The Iran-Iraq War," 129, 134.

20. Sicherman, "Iraq and Iran," 711.

21. Wright, "Implications," 288.

22. Cottam, "The Iran-Iraq War," 9–10.

23. Sicherman, "Iraq and Iran," 714–15.

24. Ibid., 712.

25. J.C. Hurewitz, "The Middle East: A Year of Turmoil," *Foreign Affairs*, 59 (1981): 563.

26. Cottam, "The Iran-Iraq War," 10.

27. William Claiborne, "Focus of Drawn-Out Gulf War Shifts Away From the Battlefield," *Washington Post* (December 7, 1980): A33.

28. Sicherman, "Iraq and Iran," 711.

29. Wright, "Implications," 286.

30. Sicherman, "Iraq and Iran," 713; Claiborne, "Focus," A33.

31. Hurewitz, "The Middle East," 564.

32. Wright, "Implications," 286.

33. Sterner, "The Iran-Iraq War," 130–31.

34. Wright,"Implications," 287.

35. Sicherman, "Iraq and Iran," 712.

36. Cottam, "The Iran-Iraq War," 9–10.

37. Drozdiak, "Iran-Iraq War," A–6.

38. Sterner, "The Iran-Iraq War," 131–32.

39. Wright, "Implications," 288.

40. Drozdiak, "Iran-Iraq War," A–6.

41. Cottam, "The Iran-Iraq War," 10.

42. Claiborne, "Focus," A33.

43. Sisco, "Middle East," 616.

44. Cottam, "The Iran-Iraq War," 12.

45. Drozdiak, "Iran-Iraq War," A–6.

46. Cottam, "The Iran-Iraq War," 10.

47. Sisco, "Middle East," 615.

48. Hurewitz, "The Middle East," 564.

49. Dennis Mullin, "For Iraq, Things Are Suddenly Looking Up," *U.S. News and World Report*, 97 (December 24, 1984): 31–32; Sterner, "The Iran-Iraq War," 132–33; and Stewart Powell and Robert Kaylor, "As Iran Seeks Decisive Victory—," *U.S. News and World Report*, 101 (September 15, 1986): 42–43.

50. Norman Friedman, "The Falklands War: Lessons Learned and Mislearned," *Orbis*, 26 (1983): 907.

51. Phil Williams, "Miscalculation, Crisis Management and the Falklands Conflict," *World Today*, 39 (1983): 148.

52. J.E.S. Fawcett, "The Falklands and the Law," *World Today*, 38 (1982): 204.

53. Guillermo A. Makin, "Argentine Approaches to the Falklands/Malvinas: Was the Resort to Violence Foreseeable?," *International Affairs*, 59 (1983): 391.

54. Ibid., 392.

55. Ibid., 391.

56. Ibid., 398–99.

57. Susan Kaufman Purcell, "War and Debt in South America," *Foreign Affairs*, 61 (1983): 662–63.

58. Friedman, "The Falklands War," 936; Williams, "Miscalculation," 146.

59. Lawrence Freedman, "The War of the Falkland Islands, 1982," *Foreign Affairs*, 61 (1982): 200.

60. Friedman, "The Falklands War," 920; Purcell, "War and Debt," 661.

61. Purcell, "War and Debt," 661–62.

62. Ibid., 662.

63. Friedman, "The Falklands War," 909.

64. Freedman, "The War," 196.

65. Friedman, "The Falklands War," 914.

66. Purcell, "War and Debt," 663.

67. Williams, "Miscalculation," 148.

68. Friedman, "The Falklands War," 908.

69. Purcell, "War and Debt," 664.

70. Friedman, "The Falklands War," 908, 936.

71. Williams, "Miscalculation," 145.

72. Purcell, "War and Debt," 663.

73. Friedman, "The Falklands War," 908.

74. Ibid., 912.

75. Williams, "Miscalculation," 144–45.

76. Freedman, "The War," 199.

77. Friedman, "The Falklands War," 910.

78. Purcell, "War and Debt," 663.

79. Friedman, "The Falklands War," 910.

80. Ibid.; Freedman, "The War," 207.

81. Friedman, "The Falklands War," 910.

82. Ibid., 908.

83. Makin, "Argentine Approaches," 401.

84. Friedman, "The Falklands War," 911.

85. Makin, "Argentine Approaches," 400.

86. Purcell, "War and Debt," 664.

87. Friedman, "The Falklands War," 911.

88. Freedman, "The War," 210.

89. Williams, "Miscalculation," 147.

90. Marci McDonald, "The Maestro of Terrorism," *Maclean's*, 97 (April 30, 1984): 31.

91. Claudia Wright, "The Prince of Paranoia," *New Statesman*, 107 (April 27, 1984): 15.

92. Ibid.

93. McDonald, "The Maestro," 31.

94. William E. Smith, "Havoc at Home, Too, for Gaddafi," *Time* 123 (May 14, 1984): 44.

95. McDonald, "The Maestro," 31.

96. Ibid.; Wright, "The Prince," 16.

97. McDonald, "The Maestro," 31.

98. Wright, "The Prince," 16.

99. Ross Laver, "Terror on a Spring Morning," *Maclean's*, 97 (April 30, 1984): 28.

100. Ibid.

101. William E. Smith, "Libya's Ministry of Fear," *Time*, 123 (April 30, 1984): 38.

102. Laver, "Terror," 28.

103. Smith, "Libya's Ministry," 36–37.

104. Angus Deming and Ronald Henkoff, "Siege in St. James's Square," *Newsweek*, 103 (April 30, 1984): 27.

105. Smith, "Libya's Ministry," 37.

106. Deming and Henkoff, "Siege," 27.

107. Russell Watson, Tony Clifton, and Theodore Stanger, "Getting Away with Murder," Newsweek, 103 (May 7, 1984): 68.

108. Smith, "Libya's Ministry," 36.

109. Laver, "Terror," 28.

110. William E. Smith, "We Want Them Out!," Time, 123 (May 7, 1984): 42–43.

111. David Lamb, "Arab World Has Better Understanding of Khadafy than West," Sunday Oregonian (December 2, 1984): E5.

112. McDonald, "The Maestro," 31; Smith, "Libya's Ministry," 36–38; Smith, "We Want Them," 42; Smith, "Havoc," 44.

113. Watson, Clifton, and Stanger, "Getting Away," 68.

114. Lamb, "Arab World," E5.

115. Smith, "We Want Them," 43.

116. Laver, "Terror," 31.

117. Smith, "We Want Them," 44.

118. Smith, "Havoc," 44.

CHAPTER 7

1. Patrick M. Morgan, Deterrence: A Conceptual Analysis (Beverly Hills, Calif.: Sage, 1977), 103.

2. Joseph Frankel, The Making of Foreign Policy: An Analysis of Decision Making (London: Oxford University Press, 1963), 172.

3. Ibid.

4. Robert Mandel, "The Desirability of Irrationality in Foreign Policy Making: A Preliminary Theoretical Analysis," Political Psychology, 5 (1984): 654.

5. David Braybrooke and Charles E. Lindblom, A Strategy of Decision (New York: Free Press, 1963); and Robert Mandel, Perception, Decision Making, and Conflict (Washington, D.C.: University Press of America, 1979), 8, 20.

6. Janice Gross Stein, "Can Decision Makers Be Rational and Should They Be? Evaluating the Quality of Decisions" in Michael Brecher, ed., Studies in Crisis Behavior (New Brunswick, N.J.: Transaction Books, 1978), 332.

7. Morgan, Deterrence, chap. 5.

8. Nigel Howard, Paradoxes of Rationality (Cambridge: MIT Press, 1971), 9.

9. Thomas C. Schelling, The Strategy of Conflict (London: Oxford University Press, 1963), 18–19.

10. Mandel, "The Desirability of Irrationality," 655.

11. Robert Jervis, *The Logic of Images in International Relations* (Princeton: Princeton University Press, 1970), chap. 5.

12. Richards J. Heuer, Jr., "Cognitive Factors in Deception and Counterdeception" in Donald C. Daniel and Katherine L. Herbig, eds., *Strategic Military Deception* (New York: Pergamon, 1982), 31–69; Richard K. Betts, *Surprise Attack: Lessons for Defense Planning* (Washington, D.C.: Brookings, 1982); and Klaus Knorr, "Strategic Surprise: The Incentive Structure" in Klaus Knorr and Patrick Morgan, eds., *Strategic Military Surprise: Incentives and Opportunities* (New Brunswick, N.J.: Transaction Books, 1983), 173–93.

13. Alexander L. George, *Presidential Decisionmaking in Foreign Policy: The Effective Use of Information and Advice* (Boulder, Colo.: Westview Press, 1980), 62–63.

14. Mandel, "The Desirability of Irrationality," 655.

15. Irving L. Janis and Leon Mann, *Decision Making* (New York: Free Press, 1977), 45.

16. Ibid., 316.

17. Morgan, *Deterrence*, 103.

18. Mandel, "The Desirability of Irrationality," 656.

19. Schelling, *The Strategy of Conflict*, 18.

20. Mandel, "The Desirability of Irrationality," 658.

CHAPTER 8

1. Yehezkel Dror, Crazy States (Millwood, N.Y.: Kraus, 1980), 63.

2. Ibid., 73–86.

3. Ibid., 87–90.

4. Ibid., 93–96.

Selected Bibliography

Allison, Graham T. *Essence of Decision*. Boston: Little, Brown, 1971.

Axelrod, Robert, ed. *Structure of Decision*. Princeton: Princeton University Press, 1976.

Benn, Stanley and G.W. Mortimore, eds. *Rationality and the Social Sciences*. London: Routledge and Kegan Paul, 1976.

Betts, Richard K. *Surprise Attack: Lessons for Defense Planning*. Washington, D.C.: Brookings, 1982.

Braybrooke, David and Charles E. Lindblom. *A Strategy of Decision*. New York: Free Press, 1963.

Downs, Anthony. *Inside Bureaucracy*. Boston: Little, Brown, 1967.

Dror, Yehezkel. *Crazy States*. Millwood, N.Y.: Kraus, 1980.

Etheredge, Lloyd S. *A World of Men: The Private Sources of American Foreign Policy*. Cambridge: MIT Press, 1978.

Frankel, Joseph. *The Making of Foreign Policy: An Analysis of Decision Making*. London: Oxford University Press, 1963.

George, Alexander L. *Presidential Decisionmaking in Foreign Policy: The Effective Use of Information and Advice*. Boulder, Colo.: Westview Press, 1980.

Goodman, Nelson. *Ways of World Making*. Indianapolis: Hackett, 1978.

Hermann, Margaret G. "Who Becomes a Political Leader? Some Societal and Regime Influences on Selection of a Head of State." In Falkowski, Lawrence S., ed. *Psychological Models in International Politics*. Boulder, Colo.: Westview Press, 1979, 15–48.

_____. "Explaining Foreign Policy Behavior: Using Personality Characteristics of Political Leaders." *International Studies Quarterly*, 24 (March 1980): 7–46.

Heuer, Richards J., Jr. "Cognitive Factors in Deception and Counterdeception." In Daniel, Donald C. and Katherine L. Herbig, eds. *Strategic Military Deception*. New York: Pergamon, 1982, 31–69.

Holsti, Ole R. *Crisis Escalation War*. Montreal: McGill-Queens University Press, 1972.

Howard, Nigel. *Paradoxes of Rationality*. Cambridge: MIT Press, 1971.

Janis, Irving L. *Victims of Groupthink*. Boston: Houghton Mifflin, 1972.

Janis, Irving L. and Leon Mann. *Decision Making*. New York: Free Press, 1977.

Jervis, Robert. *The Logic of Images in International Relations*. Princeton: Princeton University Press, 1970.

_____. *Perception and Misperception in International Politics*. Princeton: Princeton University Press, 1976.

Jones, Edward E. and Richard E. Nisbett. "The Actor and the Observer: Divergent Perceptions of the Causes of Behavior." In Jones, Edward E. and others, eds. *Attribution: Perceiving the Causes of Behavior*. Morristown, N.J.: General Learning Press, 1972, 79–94.

Kinder, Donald R. and Janet A. Weiss. "In Lieu of Rationality: Psychological Perspectives on Foreign Policy Decision Making." *Journal of Conflict Resolution*, 22 (December 1978): 707–35.

Knorr, Klaus. "Strategic Surprise: The Incentive Structure." In Knorr, Klaus and Patrick Morgan, eds. *Strategic Military Surprise: Incentives and Opportunities*. New Brunswick, N.J.: Transaction Books, 1983, 173–93.

LeVine, Robert A. and Donald T. Campbell. *Ethnocentrism*. New York: John Wiley, 1972.

Lindblom, Charles E. "The Science of 'Muddling Through'." *Public Administration Review*, 19 (Spring 1959): 79–88.

Mandel, Robert. *Perception, Decision Making, and Conflict*. Washington, D.C.: University Press of America, 1979.

_____. "The Desirability of Irrationality in Foreign Policy Making: A Preliminary Theoretical Analysis." *Political Psychology*, 5 (December 1984): 643–60.

_____. "Psychological Approaches to International Relations." In Hermann, Margaret G., ed. *Political Psychology*. San Francisco: Jossey-Bass, 1986, 251–78.

Moffitt, J. Weldon and Ross Stagner. "Perceptual Rigidity and Closure as a Function of Anxiety." *Journal of Abnormal and Social Psychology*, 52 (1956): 354–57.

Morgan, Patrick M. *Deterrence: A Conceptual Analysis*. Beverly Hills, Calif.: Sage, 1977.

Pruitt, Dean G. "Definition of the Situation as a Determinant of International Action." In Kelman, Herbert C., ed. *International Behavior*. New York: Holt, Rinehart, and Winston, 1965, 391–432.

Savage, L.J. "The Theory of Statistical Decision." *Journal of the American Statistical Association*, 46 (1951): 55–67.

Schelling, Thomas C. *The Strategy of Conflict*. London: Oxford University Press, 1963.

Simon, Herbert. "A Behavioral Model of Rational Choice." *Quarterly Journal of Economics*, 69 (1955): 99–118.

————. *Reason in Human Affairs*. Stanford: Stanford University Press, 1983.

Snyder, Glenn H. and Paul Diesing. *Conflict Among Nations*. Princeton: Princeton University Press, 1977.

Snyder, Jack L. "Rationality at the Brink: The Role of Cognitive Processes in Failures of Deterrence." *World Politics*, 30 (1978): 345–65.

Stein, Janice Gross. "Can Decision Makers Be Rational and Should They Be? Evaluating the Quality of Decisions." In Brecher, Michael, ed. *Studies in Crisis Behavior*. New Brunswick, N.J.: Transaction Books, 1978, 316–39.

Stein, Janice Gross and Raymond Tanter. *Rational Decision Making: Israel's Security Choices, 1967*. Columbus: Ohio University Press, 1980.

Steinbruner, John D. *The Cybernetic Theory of Decision*. Princeton: Princeton University Press, 1974.

Verba, Sidney. "Assumptions of Rationality and Non-Rationality in Models of the International System." In Rosenau, James N., ed. *International Politics and Foreign Policy*. Revised Edition. New York: Free Press, 1969, 217–31.

White, Ralph K. *Nobody Wanted War: Misperception in Vietnam and Other Wars*. New York: Doubleday, 1970.

Index

About the Author

ROBERT MANDEL is Associate Professor of International Affairs at Lewis and Clark College in Portland, Oregon. He is the author of *Perception, Decision Making and Conflict*.